Run Like Hell

Matt Beardshall

Published 2010 by arima publishing

www.arimapublishing.com

ISBN 978 1 84549 452 0

© Matt Beardshall 2010

arima publishing
ASK House, Northgate Avenue
Bury St Edmunds, Suffolk IP32 6BB
t: (+44) 01284 700321
www.arimapublishing.com

Acknowledgements:

An immeasurable debt of gratitude goes to Andrea, my long-suffering wife and to my children, Hannah and William. Without your unwavering support I'd never be able to attempt such ludicrously silly runs. You listen to my crazy ideas, raise an eyebrow, and shake your heads, and then let me go and torture myself anyway.

Andrea, without your courageous battle there would only be half a story - and a poorer half at that. I hope that your bravery shines like a beacon to show that there is hope and every reason to remain positive. I'm very proud of you.

June, Geoff and Kate Beardshall, Ann and Roy Stocks, Marie Slater, Cathy Butler, and Sue Southern - You gave us your time, sympathy and understanding. Thank you.

We are indebted to all the staff at Chesterfield Royal Hospital and Weston Park Hospital - especially to those in Chesterfield's Breast Unit, Imaging Department, and Cavendish Suite. There were so many magnificent individuals that it is hard to single people out, but mention has to go to Steve Holt, Dr Purohit, Jeff Glaves, Donna Ashley, and Lydia. Thanks also to our work colleagues for their support and assistance.

Many thanks go to all of team *Respect The Stupidity*: Mal Gibb, Andy Farnsworth, Vin Vanwoerkom and Justin Adams, and also to Andrea Lawton. You all think I may be the mad one, but you are equally as bonkers, if not more so. Long may it continue!

Mike 'Mad Dog' Schreiber - You are an inspiration, motivation, and guru. I hope you keep running for another 73 years.

Ken Bishton - thanks for another great wordsmith's job with the punctuation, deletions and constructive criticisms.

Anna Gilmore, you helped take my thoughts and batter them into shape. A solicitor frequenting the world of the mountain ultra-runner - run long, you crazy banana.

Thanks to the guys at The Running Bug, the friendliest running web site in the UK - Ian Knighton, John Griffith, Julia Buckley and Joe Mountain. Keep up the great work.

Thank you to Mike Gratton and staff at **209 Events** for a wonderful, well organised and truly memorable New York Marathon experience. I would happily recommend 209 events to every runner.

Lizzie Hawker, thank you for the kind words and for sharing your inspirational philosophy. You are up where I would love to be.

Thanks to all my running friends (real and virtual) for sharing the hills, trails and pavements with me.

All photographs taken by Andy Farnsworth, Andrea Beardshall and Justin Adams.

Cover photograph by Andy Farnsworth.

For Andrea, Hannah and William

Whatever you think you can do or believe you can do, begin it. Action has magic, grace, and power in it. Begin it now.

Johann Wolfgang von Goethe

What matters most in life is not the triumph, but the struggle.

Pierre de Coubertin

Facing it, always facing it, that's the way to get through life. Face it.

Joseph Conrad.

Reflections

Sunday 4th November 2007

The first few shrill beeps of my wristwatch alarm wrenched me from a deep and comfortable slumber at 5.40 am. I was out of bed and halfway through the usual morning stretching routine by the time the telephone rang to announce the pre-arranged back-up wake-up call. Today, oversleeping wasn't an option.

I had slept well considering the incessant noise from the street thirty-one floors below. The corner of Broadway and Time Square in New York epitomises the 'City That Never Sleeps'; a 24-hour traffic jam of tooting cars, unfeasibly large trucks and a myriad yellow cabs oozing slowly down a glass neon-and-steel canyon, and sharing the inadequate space with thousands of ethnically-diverse randomly-moving people. On several occasions over the previous couple of days we had heard sirens from our hotel room and gazed down to see a fire engine battling to get downtown, frantically weaving and pushing through the gridlock, rushing at a dizzying pace that must have almost reached walking speed. At other times Broadway, both north and south, appeared solid with taxi cabs, all looking like yellow cobblestones, and giving the appearance that one could step out from the window and follow the Yellow Brick Road all the way to Oz.

Not that we were initially comfortable with the bird's-eye view. This was unfamiliar territory to two people whose natural habitat was more hillside and moorland than skyscraper. We had arrived three days earlier at the Crowne Plaza Hotel at around nine pm, tired after having travelled for twenty hours. Taking the express elevator to our room made our ears pop, racing up thirty-one floors in roughly twenty seconds! On entering our room we strolled over to close a window. After the briefest of glances down we both swore and our legs buckled. Such heights were totally alien to us. It was far safer lying down on the carpet than daring to venture towards the glass with the sight of an endless plunge down into the oblivion beyond. By kneeling on all–fours the floor provided *terra firma* (it was much 'firmer' and there was much less 'terror') and we somehow managed to shut the window.

While Andrea tried to get back to sleep I prepared diligently in the half-light next to the still-closed curtains, stretching, dressing, eating and drinking sports fuel, lathering on Vaseline, and double-checking the contents of my UPS bag. This would be the only thing I would be allowed to carry on the bus to the marathon start area. Heightened security measures in post-9/11 America dictated that all marathon competitors could take only the one clear plastic bag that was provided by the organisation. Mine contained several bottles of sports drink, some energy bars and other food, more Vaseline and nip-guards, my wallet and phone, and an extra windproof jacket. One last check of all the gear and I was ready. Leaning over the bed I kissed Andrea who was snuggled down under the thick duvet, told her I'd see her later, and slipped out of the door as quietly as I could.

My eyes took a few moments to adjust to the brightness of the hotel corridor. The lift lobby area was empty and quiet, the plush carpeted floors damping any sound. As I stood my reflection stared back at me from the gleaming steel elevator doors. It was a reflection I barely recognised. I looked like a street 'hoodie' standing there in running shoes and wearing baggy trousers and a baggy sweat top with the hood pulled over my head and half-way down my face. Although I was lacking the 'bling' I thought my appearance should place me more as a rapper than a runner in mid-town Manhattan. The clothes had been bought specifically for purpose from a budget shop the day before. I needed something warm, comfortable and disposable.

I pressed the elevator-call button and waited in silence. Here, standing in the centre of one of the busiest cities in the world, about to go to the start of the biggest marathon race in the world, all seemed peaceful, and I was engulfed in a serenity that belied my surroundings. A state of relaxed calm descended. I became aware only of my slow, deep breathing, a moment of silent meditation. I was mentally ready for the race.

The 'ping' sound snapped me from the trance, the steel doors in front of me quietly hissed open, and I stepped alone into the metal box for the giddy-making 31-floor freefall down to ground level.

The same quiet hiss was repeated, but this time the opening of the lift doors threw me into a wall of noise and a scene of frantic activity. The hotel lobby was rammed with people, mostly runners, hustling in groups united by nationality. The volume of conversation was a deafening cocktail of multilingual excitement. To my right stood several Italians, all wearing matching green, white and red tracksuits. The smaller woman in their cluster spoke at a frantic, almost agitated pace, gesturing with her hands whilst the men around her nodded in enthusiastic agreement. I was able to catch the occasional word *'maratona'*. Behind them stood an orange sea of Dutch competitors. This was a larger but far less intense group, and their ethos appeared to be one of fun. Several of them sang what was evidently a humorous song, and another attempted to eat a bowl of porridge whilst his friends prodded him in the ribs and tried to pull his shorts down. The Germans stood near the windows overlooking the street, studying papers that appeared to show details of the 26.2-mile route. They were taking the business seriously, yet paradoxically most of them sported the tightest, almost comical leggings that decency laws would permit. A gathering of French runners, dressed mostly in *Le Bleu*, were slouched nonchalantly around the easy-chaired seating area, empty plates and bowls discarded on the coffee tables in front of them. They spoke little, and I wasn't sure if this was because they were nervous or confidently indifferent. Other groups gathered according to the charity for which they were running, Cancer Research in the far corner, Mencap next to the escalators.

I looked up at the huge hotel security guard who was standing by the elevators. He looked back down at me. Clearly bemused by the madness he raised a perplexed eyebrow and said, "Have a good race today, sir". I thanked him and strode into the middle of the insanity, looking for anyone I recognised.

The usual dining area was closed this early in the morning, but a meagre makeshift breakfast station had been set up in the coffee lounge. This caused a melee as hungry runners queued impatiently to stock vital energy levels. I hadn't expected any kind of food service, which is why I had snacked in our room, but I took an opportunist view and joined the queue, hopeful to acquire a bowl of porridge before having to leave with the rest of my tour group at 6.00. The plan was to walk the few blocks to the New York Library where a fleet of buses would transport runners to the marathon start area. It was made clear that the group would leave at 6.00, no later. Be there or make your own way! I wanted to be there.

At 5.50 I was still in the queue, hoping the waiter, who was handing out bagels and toast and slopping porridge into bowls at an alarming pace, would increase his work rate beyond its current frantic pace. At 5.54 I was served, and received a bowl of steaming hot gruel in one hand as I signed the cheque to charge the food to the room in the other. There were no free seats on which to sit to eat. The porridge was too hot to eat so I stood alone in a corner, blowing into the bowl, watching the time tick ever nearer 6.00, and observing the buzzing manic lunacy. I'd seen this kind of activity before – such as when you get a stick and poke an ants' nest and all the creatures rush out and become a boiling mass of randomly moving bodies and limbs, all intent on the same purpose but all getting in each other's way. This was the human equivalent. Except for the French, who just slouched!

By 6.00 I had just managed to nibble and gulp my porridge down, which must have been a humorous sight as I blew it, spooned it in, huffed and puffed and jumped about as it scalded my mouth. I sluiced it down with cold sports drink and then found my group of fellow Brits who had been initially difficult to spot as we all, collectively and individually, hid under our national camouflage of 'not-wanting-to-stand-out'. We took the escalator to ground level and walked through the doors onto Broadway.

The November air was cold and crisp and our breath steamed into the crystal-clear deep sky. The millions of stars would have been a glorious sight were it not for the giant advertising boards and video screens towering over our heads. A huge screen showed a satirical cartoon of *King Kong* in which an animated chocolate-coated *M+M* climbed the Empire State Building, thumped its chest and then panicked as it looked down and got vertigo. To the side of the video screen, through a gap in the skyscrapers, towered the real Empire State.

The city appeared exactly as I had seen it in every movie based in New York – plumes of steam burst up through the streets from the subway, yellow cabs cruised, cops sat eating donuts in black and white police cars, and men in thick coats with the collar pulled high around their ears sipped coffee whilst perched on stools in the window of cheap-looking diners. I felt as though I had fallen through a TV screen, and it was strangely exciting.

The scene from the Crowne Plaza Hotel was being repeated in all directions. Clusters of fit-looking men and women, all dressed in warm but sporty clothes and clutching the same UPS bag, walked briskly toward the same destination. The street 'grid' system used in Manhattan meant that each group could take a slightly different route through the criss-cross, either walking parallel to each other, or crossing paths before turning in the same direction. Closer to the library the factions started to cluster, but it wasn't until we turned the final corner at Fifth Avenue that the sheer enormity of the event hit home.

Lined up on the roadside outside the library were more buses than I could quickly count. In fact, counting was impossible as buses were pulling out of the line and driving away only to be replaced immediately by others from a seemingly endless queue of vehicles that had built up along the street behind me. The number of passengers was equally impressive. Thousands of athletes were lined along the wide pavement, being ushered towards the buses by loud and enthusiastic stewards armed with megaphones. The efficiency was remarkable. The queue moved at walking pace as runners were encouraged to jump on any available bus.

And there were even spectators here, cheering and chanting, waving flags, psyching up all the competitors and wishing us good luck and a great race. If this were a taste of the support to come then the New York marathon would be quite some experience. It was hard not to get carried away, but with the start of the race still over three-and-a-half hours away I endeavoured to keep a lid on my excitement and remain calm and focused.

This was the last point where non-runners could accompany competitors. Possession of a race number was the passport onto a bus. I was hurried to the very front vehicle and climbed aboard behind two Scottish runners with whom I had chatted as we walked. Within a minute the bus pulled away leaving the cheering melee behind, the rowdiness replaced by calmer conversation that, although in many different languages, was all clearly related to the same subject: running the New York marathon.

The bus initially headed downtown and we had excellent views of the Empire State Building, the top few floors of which were becoming illuminated by the fiery orange glow of the rising sun, now in front and to my left, blazing its way fiercely into a crisp morning, reflecting from steel and glass, highlighting steam wispily escaping from vents and chimneys, painting buildings in its brilliance, and illuminating an exodus of crowded coaches, all heading for Staten Island. The trip would take over half an hour.

I closed my eyes, took several deep breaths, and in a state of profound relaxation began thinking of how Andrea and I had managed to make it all the way to New York. Not in the physical sense, but the emotional and philosophical journey from the last big running adventure eighteen months ago, through the cancer and the chemotherapy, the drugs and the nausea. Through time spent running and time spent fighting, through triumph and disaster, through near-death running on wild hills, through exhaustion and through serene calm and peaceful togetherness. It probably went unnoticed, but sitting quietly on that bus I was welling up with more emotion than I had experienced for a long time. Life's an ultra-marathon. Together Andrea and I had battled through 'the wall' and we were still running. We had much to be thankful for.

***

An Ending; A Beginning

I glanced at the clock. It was just after three in the morning as I hobbled painfully into the hotel bathroom, carrying Hannah as she continued vomiting. Both of us, and the bed sheet, were covered in the stuff as I bobbed down, wincing from the pain in my knee, and lowered her into the bath, still retaining unpleasant remnants of our four-year-old daughter's evening meal. This was the third time she'd been sick during this night and, after turning on the taps to refill the bath, I slumped to the floor, utterly exhausted, and longed for rest. Andrea, my wife, couldn't help. She was engaged in her own nocturnal battle with our five-month-old son, William, who was also sleeping badly and requiring all-too-frequent night feeds.

I washed Hannah as she sat sobbing in the warm soapy water. Behind me, screwed up on the floor lay an ever-increasing pile of rolled-up bedding that gave off a stomach-churning aroma. I dried her, dressed her in clean clothes and lifted her into the double bed currently occupied by Andrea, with William lying on her chest.

"Gee, thanks", Andrea muttered sarcastically, but Hannah's bed was unusable now and I had nowhere else to put her.

By the time I had re-cleaned the bath the insipid glow of the bathroom light was losing its battle with the oncoming dawn that was trying to sneak in through the curtains. Sliding gently into bed between wife and daughter I resigned myself to the fact that this would be a night with very little sleep. My coast-to-coast fantasy had been shattered in the cruellest way. What I wanted most after completing a gruelling 180-mile run across northern England was a damned good night's sleep. Instead, I felt simply that we'd been damned. Barely twelve hours had passed since we'd finished and the challenge had proved to be an unpredictable beast.

In the preceding week I had run a mountainous marathon distance every day to complete an off-road crossing of the full width of northern England. But this hadn't been without incident, and my team-mate Vin and I both sported very painful injuries.

The five of us in the team – myself and Vin as runners, Mal who mountain-biked, and our support crew of Andy and Justin – had begun the seven-day ultra-marathon in high spirits, messing about in the glorious sunshine of the Cumbrian coast. Despite the heat, the terrain, and the long distances, the first two days had been easier than we expected, and we crossed the magnificent Lake District with barely a hitch. But as we progressed on eastwards, things became steadily harder and more serious, and this seemed to have been reflected in the worsening weather.

Vin had developed a thigh injury that ultimately resulted in his failure to complete the entire journey on foot. In a difficult day for the support crew, he was driven back to the point where he'd been forced to abandon his run, and he made up the lost distance by riding a spare bike. He managed to join me to run the last day to the finish. Both of us were in agony and full of painkillers, hobbling under a mournful sky that sobbed heavy rain through a handkerchief of low, thick cloud.

What began as an ultra-fun-run had ultimately become a serious endeavour, but it had been an incredible and emotional quest. We had run through high mountains and fantastic scenery, met colourful characters, and had close encounters with all manner of wildlife – deer, wild parrots, and even wilder bulls. Mal had even biked through a field of sheep that he described as "Hitchcockian": the beasts surrounded him in a sinister and threatening manner and refused to move.

All my family and several friends had been in Robin Hood's Bay to see us finish, and this, combined with the prolonged physical exertion, resulted in an outpouring of emotion the like of which I had never experienced. I had enjoyed the athletic and emotional intoxication of high adventure. Now I was suffering the hangover.

Everybody was gathered around the dining table when Andrea, the children and I finally made it down for breakfast, bleary-eyed and exhausted. The dining room picture-windows offered a fantastic view over the manicured hotel lawn and down to the bay below. The visibility was intermittently limited by a swirling sea fret, as if a giant magician was performing smoke-and-mirror trickery with the coastline.

The mood at the table was joyful, almost celebratory, following the success, albeit painful, of our seven-day passage from west coast to east. Vin sat next to Ans, his mother. Both of them were enjoying the excellent breakfast. Vin, despite not carrying an ounce of body fat, has the ability to consume his own weight in food during a decent meal. He looked like he was revving up for his greatest ever intake of bacon and eggs. His thigh was still very sore but not causing him anywhere near as much pain as my knee. I'd had to limp slowly along the corridors of The Raven Hall Hotel, and hop in agony down the stairs to get to the dining room.

Next to Vin sat Mal and his partner, also called Andrea, both looking extremely relaxed. But then 'relaxed' should be Mal's middle name. His epic mountain-bike journey had been smooth, calculated and controlled (although very tough), and the only time he was seen to flap was when a hot cup of tea had accidentally been poured over his genitals.

Justin and Andy were tucking into large plates of 'full English' breakfast while discussing the relative merits of some camera gadgetry. The two of them seemed to inhabit a strange world somewhere between that of human beings and gadget-driven cyborgs. To the rest of us on the team, their technobabble conversations were unintelligible, but when it came to locating us in the wilderness and slapping a cup of tea and some cake in our hands, just when we needed it most, their ability was uncanny.

Sitting next to the three empty seats that awaited our occupation were my parents who were expecting to take Hannah home with them. This would allow Andrea and me the chance to recover from the run. Hannah's sickness bug had put paid to that. It wasn't fair to send them away with an ill child. I would have to find some other time to recuperate from the multi-day ultra-marathon we had completed not 24 hours previously. I felt utterly exhausted and knew that today would be an ordeal.

With breakfast finished the group started to disperse. Before heading home Vin and Ans had a relaxing stroll around the grounds of the hotel that stood proudly on the cliff-top overlooking the North Sea. Built on the site of a fifth-century Roman fort, Raven Hall stands behind spectacular battlements, 600-feet above the sea, from which there are dramatic views towards the small fishing village of Robin Hood's Bay where we had ended our ultra-marathon.

My optimism during its early stages had led me to believe that Vin and I would complete the run on foot all the way to the hotel. We wanted to avoid setting foot in a car. Such thoughts were dashed 100 miles into our journey when our injuries really kicked-in.

My parents left soon after Vin and Ans. It had been wonderful having them with us to boost morale on the final day. Not surprisingly, Hannah made a remarkably rapid full recovery within 30 minutes of their driving away. Half an hour before, she was white as a blanched banshee. As though revived by the wand-wave of a fairy godmother, the colour returned to her cheeks, impish life flooded back into her youthful body, and she wanted to play, play, play. Oh joy! I was injured, exhausted, sleep-deprived and now the guardian of an overactive, running, dancing, mischievously normal four-year-old whose non-stop activity conformed to the *chaos theory*.

Andrea headed back to bed for much-needed sleep while the rest of us took the children to play in the rock pools at nearby Boggle Hole. They loved it, but my mood was flat, and physically I felt as though I had a terrible hangover on top of jetlag. I should have been elated at our team's endurance endeavours and I was annoyed at my sour disposition.

The weather was *in simpatico* as thick clouds hung overhead, blocking out the warm sunlight that should have shone on our lap of victory. Drizzle fell like tears of frustration at the depressingly deflating anticlimax. And there was the physical pain. My left knee stung fiercely with every step. "Don't do any permanent damage," I had said over and over to myself as I'd hobbled the last few days. I was starting to think that I'd never run injury-free again.

After a casual day the team finally said their farewells and everyone headed back to their homes and 'normal' lives. Work, routine and domesticity did its best to fill the void left by the coast-to-coast adventure.

It failed miserably!

***

I returned to my dayjob to a fair amount of interest from my colleagues and friends. I was not so much a minor celebrity for being daft enough to run 180-miles, more a major curiosity. And my obvious heavy limp prevented any self-assured exaggerations about whether I had found it easy or not.

I soon contacted my coach and mentor, Mike 'Mad Dog' Schreiber, to fill him in with the details of our ultra-marathon exploits. Although I had never met him, I felt like we were friends. I only conversed with Mad Dog via email as he lives, and runs, in the mountains of Mexico. Having covered super-long distances for over 50 years, and still running them in his seventies, his knowledge and experience were invaluable to me. I pictured him as a tough, no-nonsense guy, shaped, tempered and hardened by his lifestyle and environment, living 'close to the edge', but always in control, rather like Vitruvian Man mixed with Bear Grylls.

Mad Dog got the full coast-to-coast story. His reply was swift. He informed me that had I been able to email him during the run he would have been able to offer advice to help prevent the knee condition worsening.

He recommended wearing a 'patella band', a strap that is positioned below the kneecap to provide support while walking or running. I promptly acquired one, put it on, and it felt good. Not perfect, but a big improvement. Walking on the flat and uphill was mostly pain-free, but hobbling downstairs remained agony.

But Mad Dog was pleasingly positive in his response to the endeavour. I asked him if I could now call myself an Ultra-runner. He replied that I was most definitely an Ultra-runner, and more than that, ours was "a true adventure to rival the pioneers of old". Praise indeed from a man who has been running trail ultra-marathons for more than 50 years.

Andy planned to edit a video of the coast-to-coast, but realised that he didn't have enough action film of Mal biking. So the two of them met up in the Peak District, Andy strapped his tiny video camera to Mal's bike, and set him off down a favourite, fast downhill trail near to Ladybower reservoir.

Mal had ridden this trail many times before, always launching his bike around the sharp gritty corners and over the many rocks that protruded through the path, and always getting to the bottom with a big grin on his face. This time the bike launched Mal.

Half way down the trail he took to the air over a grassy hump, but didn't land well. The front wheel twisted and stopped dead, but Mal didn't. A second flight took him over the handlebars Superman-style, and into the rocks and heather. His left collarbone was in pieces. Sharp shards of it threatened to pierce the skin between neck and shoulder. Less significant, but equally impressive, was the black tread pattern of one of his tyres imprinted all the way down his thigh and calf, having the appearance of a large traditional Maori tattoo.

Andy scuttled down the hill to help him, scooped up the bits (of man and machine) and drove him to hospital in Huddersfield. X-Rays showed the collarbone to be in a mess. Mal would be out of action for a long time. (To this day, conspiracy theories surround the accident. It happened just as the 2006 football World Cup started. Mal saw every game!)

I hadn't broken any bones but I was still unable to run. To occupy spare time I began to type out an account of the coast-to-coast run. I had scribbled some notes on scrap paper as we had made our way from west to east, really just a few sentences describing the major events and feelings from each day. I intended to produce a diary of our exploits, merely a personal reminder. It was surprising to discover how much detail I could remember, and even more surprising to find I enjoyed the writing. The account steadily expanded.

I really had no idea where my 'diary' was going to take me.

Two weeks passed before my knee was comfortable in normal activity. The limp had vanished, and walking downstairs was painless. In fact, walking anywhere was effortless. My fitness and endurance levels were sky-high. I felt light, fit and athletic. Training for and running the coast-to-coast had done me the world of good. Now was the time to prove that I hadn't done any permanent damage. It was time to try running.

***

First Steps

I returned home from work on a glorious day in late May. The world was as it should be - bright sunlight, a cheerful evening, leaves dancing and birds surfing on the light breeze. Donning my favourite running shorts and vest, I stepped out of the front door, patella band firmly under my left kneecap.

The first few steps were merely a gentle jog and, although pain-free, this was mental torture nevertheless. I was waiting for the thunderbolt to strike my left leg. It never came. I slowly increased my pace, convinced this would be agonising. It wasn't. I started to relax, and by the time I had covered over a mile I was running almost at my normal pace.

No pain! I could hardly believe it. I felt fantastic. It was a beautiful day and I was back to the special place that fills my mind with tranquillity and my body with elation-inducing endorphins. Thoughts jostled in my head - where should I run? Maybe into the woods? How about up the hill and into the Peak District? How about knocking off a quick half-marathon?

I was like a child heading for the sweetshop with a fistful of pocket money, mindful of the parental dictum: "Don't spend it all at once". I allowed common sense to reign in the delirium. Today was about testing my recovery, not my limits. I eased back a little and plotted a route of about three miles. Returning home still free of pain, I grinned delightedly to myself. I could run again. I planned to do lots more of it.

By July I was back to my normal running routine and the patella band had been relegated to the first aid kit. The distances I covered were steadily increasing, along with my speed. I was training sensibly, and really enjoying it, but the summer just seemed to be passing by aimlessly. It was fun, but something was missing.

Running an ultra-marathon had proved to be a dangerous thing. Like a naïve youth after his first hit of heroin - "I'll try it just once more" -, I was slipping into addiction and already looking for my next fix. I read a quote somewhere that the difference between a jogger and a runner was that a jogger still has control over their lives. I was a runner.

I was training well, but for what? Sure, there were the local races – 10km and half-marathons, and in fact I had my eye on the Worksop half-marathon in October - but I felt like I was trying to hold back the adventure. My regular little runs couldn't plug the leaks in the dam of my desire for another really big challenge. The dam felt like it was about to burst.

Mal was also missing the adventure of his coast-to-coast mountain biking, but he had no way of releasing his energy and frustrations. His collarbone steadfastly refused to heal. Eight weeks after his crash he was still unable to run, swim or ride. To help ease our mental turmoil we began to exchange emails, bouncing around ideas for another challenge.

***

July eased itself casually into the comfort of August, and Andrea, who had wanted to increase her own level of exercise, casually eased herself into running. This was the third time she had started a running program. In June 2001 she had been running three or four times a week before Hannah was conceived. In the spring of 2005 her running was again curtailed, this time by William's conception. Surely it would be third time lucky? With the short-term aim of completing a 10km race, she bought herself a new pair of running shoes and signed up with Mad Dog for a training schedule tailored to her requirements.

She didn't enjoy the activity quite as much as I did, which makes her dedication and commitment in sticking to the program even more impressive. One Tuesday evening she was scheduled to cover four miles. It had been raining very heavily on and off all day. Even though the downpours seemed to have eased, heavy, black clouds were looming overhead as she prepared to set out.

The god Thor must still be angry, I thought, and it was clear that another storm was brewing. No one would have blamed Andrea had she decided to sit this one out. I'm not sure I would have been keen to venture out, but she laced up her shoes, kissed us all goodbye, and jogged away into the eerie gloom. The air was still and dark and felt charged with electricity, like a mugger lurking in the shadows, waiting to strike. This was clearly the calm before the storm. Five minutes later the tempest hit - hard.

It began with raindrops large enough to strike the ground like falling stones, and the light dimmed to a blue-blackness. A murmuring sound built up to a deafening hiss as the clouds wrung themselves dry. Millions of marble-sized raindrops pounded the ground. Debris was washed into the road and whirled about as it rode the rapids down into the culverts. Several times Thor's hammer swung and pounded the air with a boom that resonated in the pit of the stomach.

And through it all Andrea kept running. After half an hour the storm's full fury was spent. It loosened its stranglehold and dispersed, like a pride of lions, fully sated and sloping off to sleep in the shade after a feeding frenzy. I was looking through the kitchen window, wondering how she was faring, when she appeared round the corner with her hands on her hips. Water dripped from every limb and her hair was plastered to her head. Her face was glowing and a few wisps of steam rose from her body as from a racehorse after a hard gallop. I expected her to be really cross, but she wore a big grin and had a twinkle in her eye that suggested, "I really enjoyed that. I stuck it out, rode the storm and saw the job through. I won!" I was very proud of her.

Andrea worked hard to maintain her running schedule during our family holiday. We rented a cottage in Sleights, near Whitby in North Yorkshire, and took Andrea's mother, Ann, and stepfather, Roy, with us. The cottage was in a wonderful location with fantastic views westwards up the Esk valley to the North York Moors. But this was a torment for me. From the cottage I could see the paths that Vin and I had traversed on the coast-to-coast. One section between Hecks Wood and Back Wood was tantalisingly close.

I couldn't stop looking at them and reliving the adventure, but it was like prodding an open wound. I was torturing myself. Partial relief came from accompanying Andrea on her training runs, just as at home. We even took a push-along trailer that the children could ride in so they could join us, but the yearning for another big run grew ever stronger.

***

Respect The Stupidity

The summer tired and released its grip on the leaves that meandered playfully to the ground, laying a golden brown carpet over the roads and tracks in Clumber Park. The Worksop half-marathon was 13.1 miles of undulating forest scenery and it offered the potential to achieve a 'personal best'. And a personal best was exactly what I wanted. Despite having run the distance in under 90 minutes in training, I wanted an official 'sub 1:30' half-marathon time. The weather was perfect: cool, dry and clear with the promise of some late season sunshine. Most importantly there was little wind.

Having previously covered the course, I remembered a long straight section between miles 10 and 12 that was usually run in the teeth of the prevailing wind. Blustery days could rapidly flatten the batteries of a body weary from already having run for an hour. I also recalled that the only significant uphill section was at the end of the first mile, so setting off too fast would be ill-advised. Last time, having paced too quickly up the hill, I suffered the psychological torment of having to slow down, and seeing hundreds of more sensible runners streaming past me. I never recovered from the mistake and ended up battling through a painful ordeal to finish just outside my target time at 1 hour 32 minutes.

When we run slowly and easily our bodies utilise fat as the predominant fuel source. There is a plentiful supply of this, even in very thin people, and we can continue plodding along, cooking on a low heat, for many hours. As we increase the intensity of running, the glycogen stored in the muscles is required to power the effort. There is only a limited supply of this. When it is used up the power dramatically decreases as the body is forced to resort to fat usage once more. Running out of muscle glycogen is unpleasant to varying degrees depending upon the extent of depletion, and has acquired the term 'bonking'. Depending on the level of training and preparation, and the speed of running, glycogen stores typically last in the region of 90 minutes: run harder and it is used up more quickly, slow down and it lasts longer, but so does the race.

There are many other important physiological factors involved, (for example the rates of lactic acid production and clearance, and oxygen metabolism), but at my target running pace for the half-marathon my glycogen stores would be depleted around the time I expected to finish the race. I had a delicate balancing act to perform to achieve my goal.

This time I devised a strategy. On uphill sections I would shorten my stride but speed up my stepping rate. Then I'd run a comfortably hard pace that was sustainable on the flats. On the downhill sections I would lean forward and open my stride and let gravity pull me onwards as quickly and smoothly as possible. In this way I'd hope to have enough energy left in the tank to go hard back down the hill to the finish.

It was all planned out in my mind, but I couldn't help feeling some nervousness as I parked the car 300 yards from the start area. I slid over to the passenger seat to stick on nip-guards and apply Vaseline to my feet - I didn't want any chafing. I then climbed out to have a warm-up jog and stretch before lining up with the massed throngs of amateur athletes. Several feet behind me another man was doing likewise. He caught my eye as his running clothes were much older-looking than everyone else's. There were no modern fibres or bright colours, his shorts were long and baggy and resembled military issue, and his green woollen top I guessed had seen too many races back in the 1950s.

He was remarkably supple and fit for someone who was well into his seventies, possibly eighties. He had a wide array of flexible moves, and not a bad swagger as he stopped the stretching and jogged towards the start. I was immensely impressed, and found myself hoping three things. I hoped he finished the race, I hoped he didn't beat me, and I hoped one day to be just like him and able to complete 13 miles at such a mature age. If he were a French cheese he would have been very expensive!

As is usual with road races, the start area was a busy bustling crowd of runners all packed into a narrow lane. Along the road were 'estimated finishing time' markers, which provided some idea as to where each runner ought to position him or herself in the pack. Right at the front were the 'Under 1 hr.15 min.' whippets and greyhounds, not an ounce of fat amongst them, all fired up and looking tense and ready, as if straining at the leash in eagerness to set off. Behind them the competitors all looked like serious runners, but the general atmosphere was slightly more informal. Quiet conversation and friendly banter rippled pleasantly through the ranks. This was the 'Under 1:30' section, and I eased myself into this crowd close to the right hand kerb, apologising to one or two people as I accidentally nudged them while trying to squeeze in.

Peering around at the heads and faces swarming together, I couldn't see the stretchy old man. He was surely further back down the line of over a thousand runners. Despite the clear, sunny sky, it was still a cool morning, consistent with late October, and I wasn't the only person shivering slightly in the underdressed state of shorts and a running vest. In fact, we were all huddled together in the manner of a large flock of penguins on the Antarctic ice. The crowd warmed those in the middle, while those at the edges shivered and tried to shuffle inwards to escape the cold.

A nostril-clearing aroma of 'Deep Heat' wafted through the crisp air. Up at the front, under the Start gantry, someone - possibly the Mayor of Worksop - began to address the crowd. His voice was difficult to hear, except by the whippets who were probably too preoccupied with the imminent sprint from the traps to listen to the message. There was a ramshackle countdown from ten to zero, a horn sounded and the whippets leapt forward in a mass of bright vests and skinny arms and legs. You could well imagine them howling and barking, like a pack of huskies pulling a sled. The rest of us shuffled forwards slowly for a few seconds then began to jog before running under the gantry and off towards the forest.

A hundred yards from the start the road turned 90-degrees to the left. I kept my position at the edge of the tide of runners, hugging the right-hand kerb. Andrea and the children had come to watch the start and the finish of the race, and we had pre-arranged that they would stand on the right-hand footpath, just beyond the bend. Sure enough, there they were, Andrea standing behind the pushchair in which William slept while Hannah jumped around, holding her mother's hand.

Andrea saw me approaching and pointed me out. Hannah bounced around even more excitedly. We waved and blew kisses to each other as I passed, and I tried to shout, "I love you!" to them, but I was surprisingly emotional and it came out all quiet and croaky. I have no idea whether they heard or not.

I soon settled into a good rhythm, making sure faster runners didn't pull me along too quickly, holding the pace back up the climb at the end of the first mile. Over the brow of the hill the route took a right turn onto a wider road. I could see the whippets bounding along two or three hundred yards ahead, and between them and me were 50 or 60 runners in a wide line of bouncing heads and swinging arms.

Unlike on the previous occasion I felt good after the first mile, and found myself moving gradually forward through the ranks. I stuck to my plan all the way, trying to relax and not look at my watch for fear of getting stressed about my pace. By the fifth mile any pre-race chills had completely vanished. The sun was higher in the sky, and its warming effect could be felt through the trees under which we ran. A few leaves fluttered downwards, as if trying to get involved with the action.

After the tenth mile I was more in danger of overheating than getting cold, and I was still running strongly through this usually windy section. I risked a glance at my watch at the 12-mile marker, hoping the last mile wouldn't require an all-out sprint to achieve my target. It read 1 hour 20 minutes. I was delighted, knowing that all I had to do was maintain a steady pace to beat my personal best. But I didn't maintain a steady pace. I increased it.

I flew down the short hill and then pumped my tired, wobbly legs back into town. I rounded the last bend into the finishing straight and heard Andrea and Hannah shouting at me from behind the barriers. They were waving and trying to take a photograph. I waved back as I continued my sprint finish, and crossed the line as the clock on the gantry read 1:26:08. I had achieved my goal and was now a 'sub 1:30' half-marathon runner.

I was still spluttering and gasping for breath through a wide, happy grin when Andrea and Hannah grabbed me in the finishing area. We shared a few sweaty hugs before collecting my race-finisher's T-shirt and heading off to Ann's for Sunday lunch. The food tasted even better than usual.

What of the stretchy septuagenarian? I had no idea how long he took to complete the course, or whether he even finished the race, but he certainly started it, and that is worthy of great recognition. His efforts showed that age is not necessarily a bar to physical endurance or personal sporting ambition. All that is needed is the commitment to train and prepare, and the belief that one *can* achieve what many consider unachievable. Belief, commitment and preparation are the key words. "Can't" is a powerfully negative word, overused by the masses who live to their expectations; if you expect to have limited mobility in your later years then you most probably will have. However, with belief, commitment and preparation you can create your own reality, achieve great feats, and swim against the tide of age-related decline.

Mr Stretchy Septuagenarian had life nailed. This was not a one-off event for him. He'd clearly lived life this way. The quote at the beginning of this book sums it up.

Whatever you think you can do or believe you can do, begin it. Action has magic, grace, and power in it. Begin it now.

The fit old chap left an indelible mark on me. Did I want to run half-marathons at the age of 70?

You bet! More than that, I wanted, by his age, still to be running ultra-marathons!

***

Andrea's training was going well. She was now comfortably running every step of five miles, and gradually increasing the distances covered during each week. She was looking trim and fit, and feeling great as well. Now confident in her abilities she set her sights on the Bolsover 10K. The 10km (6.1) mile route of this race is slightly undulating but without any significant hills. Coach Mad Dog had no doubts about her ability. He told her that she'd have no trouble completing the race and that, by following his program, success in the event was a 'done deal'. I planned to run the event alongside her, so we both entered.

Although this was another run to look forward to it would be short and slow by my usual standards, and I craved more than this. I could resist the ultra-addiction no longer, and finally succumbed to some 'serious run' planning.

For months I had been throwing ideas around in my head about a potential sequel to the coast-to-coast. Something significant! The problem was the coast-to-coast had appeared so aesthetically perfect that it seemed impossible to come up with an original idea to trump it. How could we beat something that had well-defined start and finish points, crossed the entire width of the country, followed an iconic walking route, climbed numerous mountains and fells through three National Parks, and which fitted neatly into the concept of 'seven marathons in seven days'.

I knew tales of surfers spending years searching for the 'perfect wave', bobbing around on the sea, studying weather and tide charts, and looking for ocean storms just to get that once-in-a-lifetime ride on a wave of mystical magnificence. I could understand how they felt.

The idea of running from Land's End to John O'Groats (known as 'LEJOG', or 'end to end') was raised by several people, but this was ruled out as being too long to fit in with our currently busy work and home lives. Other long distance footpaths, such as the Pennine Way and Offa's Dyke path were also considered, but none seemed quite right for one reason or another.

Then there were the organised major international ultra-marathons to consider, such as the Marathon des Sables (which crosses the Sahara), but these seemed too...well...popular and organised. Something independent, unusual and preferably original would be the ideal.

But there was another significant factor. Running the coast-to-coast had meant that Andrea had been alone with both our young children for a week, and she was understandably very reluctant to repeat the tiring situation.

After several discussions and exchanges of emails with Mal and the rest of our '*Respect The Stupidity*' team, it was decided that this year we'd set our sights elsewhere and go for a smaller but still significant one-day challenge, one on which our respective other-halves could accompany us. As it would be the year of my 40th birthday, a challenge of 40 miles seemed appropriate.

During my trawls through information regarding long distance footpaths I had read about the Lyke Wake Walk. Although at just 43-miles it was initially shorter than I had hoped for in a challenge, the Lyke Wake had a romantic and mysterious history that struck a chord deep within, one that began to resonate and excite me to the point where I knew I just had to run it. This was a challenge for those full of life, borne from the belief in ancient Yorkshire that, after a person's death, the soul had to make a long and arduous journey over Whinny Moor before going to heaven. The body (the 'Lyke') was laid out at home overnight before burial, and a wake held. During this time a fire and a candle had to remain lit, and a traditional dirge sung. A woman at the wake of a dead body would sing the Cleveland 'Lyke Wake Dirge', probably the oldest dialect verse known. This was common practice until around the year 1624. The last recorded singing was around the year 1800. After the soul had completed its journey the body could finally be buried.

In 1955 Bill Cowley, a man who had spent his life living and working on the Yorkshire Moors, mused at the fact that a person can walk for days across the heather without seeing another soul, having only sheep and grouse for company. He issued a challenge for anyone to walk across the North Yorkshire Moors from Osmotherly, at the western edge to Ravenscar, on the east coast, within a time limit of 24 hours. This route ensures a crossing of the moors at their widest and highest points, taking in numerous steep valleys and gulleys. In that 43 miles there is over 5,000 feet of ascent and descent. He immediately became the first person to complete the challenge, and the Lyke Wake Walk was born.

Shortly after that, the Lyke Wake Club was initiated. Anyone successfully completing the challenge is eligible to be a club member. Male members take the name 'Dirgers', while female members are 'Witches'. There is so much steep climbing and descending along the Lyke Wake route that the profile resembles a seismograph reading, and it passes numerous ancient tumuli and burial grounds. These commonly carry the name *howe*. Many are still visible as a hump in the earth, known as a 'barrow'.

Built mostly in the Stone Age, barrows are generally associated with burial remains, and were usually rectangular or trapezoid in shape. Many face eastwards, and once contained stone or wooden mortuary chambers that remained open for many years for the deposition or removal of remains and artefacts. It was believed that any article given away in kindness during life would be returned to the donor in the spirit world following their death, and that this article could be used to aid their final long and arduous journey to the afterlife. Shoes, clothing and food would have been popular gifts. At some point the barrows were sealed and covered with earth, leaving the mounds visible today.

With this mix of history, mystique and a tough physical challenge, it sounded like the perfect run. I was pleased to find there is an annual Lyke Wake Race on the nearest Saturday to the 10th July.

At last, a plan emerged. It was pencilled in as the next challenge, and a worthy one at that. The run would involve periods of isolation, desolation, and plenty of navigation, as well as stamina, strength and a steely determination.

There is an official guidebook to the Lyke Wake Walk which says to expect "rain, cold, and wet peat bogs. Anything better is a bonus." Surely not in mid-July, when we had scheduled our attempt! Apart from the first two miles the whole route is on exposed high moorland. There would be no shelter from the elements, especially the summer sun. The more I thought about the Lyke Wake, the more concerned I became about the possibility of sunburn.

Camaraderie had been a vital ingredient in the successful coast-to-coast recipe, and I hoped for the Lyke Wake to be a similar team effort. Recruiting the team was easy. Mal was immediately enthusiastic about biking across the North York Moors, assuming his collarbone would heal. Vin, with his usual enthusiasm, declared the challenge to be "Brilliaaaaaaant". Andy went immediately into techno-overdrive, babbling about gadgets and widgets that he could use to simplify, complicate or just have fun with on the moors. Justin also declared himself 'in', and even briefly mentioned getting his bike out again (it having been retired after a small cameo role in the coast-to-coast). Team *Respect the Stupidity* was all set to ride again.

***

By November Andrea's preparations for the Bolsover 10K were well on track. She was almost covering the six-mile distance on her longer runs, and was also working on increasing her speed with some shorter, faster mid-week training sessions. Despite cooler temperatures during late autumn there was plenty of uplifting sunshine. She found this to be elevating and enriching, and she was energised by exercising in the fresh air.

Hannah, William and I often accompanied her, the children riding in the trailer as I pushed them along. William, nearing his first birthday, sometimes used the trips to catch up on some much-needed sleep. Hannah, by contrast, being a typical four-and-a-half-year-old, loved to expend as much energy as she could. She regularly jumped out of the trailer and ran alongside her mum before tiring and leaping back in the trailer for a rest.

It was all great fun, and sometimes a little noisy with laughter, children's squeals and the occasional cheery shout to one another. We'd get back home from the trips and play on the front lawn while Andrea stretched before heading to the shower.

On returning from just such a run, life felt good. We were having a great time as a family. The kids were giggling and rolling in the grass. I chased them around the tree and swung them in the air. Andrea stood listening to the fun and laughter cheerfully wafting through the bathroom window as she recovered from the joyful outing. Then, while washing, she felt a lump in her right breast.

***

Andrea

The lump was on the outer edge of her right breast, almost under the armpit. We weren't initially concerned. Andrea had only recently stopped breast-feeding William, and she was advised that some lumpiness in the breast tissue was to be expected. But a few days later she sensed that it was increasing in size.

At the time she was fortunate to be working in the Breast Screening Unit at the local hospital. She went to see the breast consultant, Steve Holt, and asked his opinion. He invited her into his consulting room to check it out.

Mr Holt examined her and raised an eyebrow, saying that the lump needed further investigation. An ultrasound examination was immediately arranged. Andrea was well acquainted with Jeff Glaves, the consultant radiologist who performed the scan, as she had previously been his personal secretary. Dr Glaves remained poker-faced throughout the examination. This was not a comfortable situation for either of them. She was having her breast scanned by her former boss, and he was in the difficult position of potentially having to make a serious diagnosis on a friend and work colleague.

After a few minutes scrutinising the monitor, Dr Glaves informed Andrea that a biopsy was required – a needle had to be inserted into the breast and a sample of the tissue removed for laboratory analysis. Although painful for Andrea this was done with the minimum of fuss. At the end of the procedure he left the room to speak to Mr Holt.

Andrea was recalled into the surgeon's consulting room. His assessment of the lump was that it was 'suspicious'. He couldn't add any further information until the biopsy results were back.

I was off work with a tummy bug that day. It was lunchtime when the telephone rang. Andrea was on the other end of the line, and it was clear that something was wrong. She wasn't crying, but her voice was trembling and solemn. She slowly described the events as they had happened, and repeated the word 'suspicious'.

"Suspicious."

OK, so he hadn't said 'bad' or 'cancer', but Andrea and I were both thinking the same thing – Mr Holt had enough experience to know what was good and what was bad. 'Suspicious' assumed 'cancer' unless proved otherwise by the biopsy. The sample results would normally take four or five days.

A mere two days later we were sitting in his consulting room, in the smart and newly-built extension to the Breast Unit. A large window cast light into the clinically furnished space. On the other side of the window was a landscaped courtyard, with a few new bushes trying to haul themselves up the wooden lattice fence. The room was bright but not so the mood. Steve Holt had also taken part in the Worksop half-marathon, and we often had brief chats about our running plans when we passed in the hospital corridors. Also present was Donna Ashley, the breast care nurse - enthusiastic, knowledgeable and very friendly. Maybe the fact that we were all colleagues made the moment more difficult. Would it have been easier if we were all strangers? I squeezed Andrea's hand as the results were explained. The consultant was sympathetic and supportive. He delivered the facts directly and with no scientific waffle. The lump was a cancer.

There it was - the word. Six small letters morphing into a great ball of lead that dropped to the floor as from a cannon, pulling our stomachs down with it. My heart raced, my face flushed, and I choked back my feelings. I couldn't imagine how it must have been for Andrea.

Mr Holt continued, explaining that the growth was quite aggressive and would have to be removed promptly, along with some of the lymph nodes that were under Andrea's arm. The cannonball smashed through the floor and plunged into the basement.

A date for the surgery had already been arranged: Friday 8th

December 2006

There are times when it is right to run, and times when you *have* to run. But there are some things you can't run away from. Sometimes you have to stop running and stand and fight.

***

We had to tell our families about Andrea's diagnosis. But how do you do that? What is the easiest way to say, "Mum, I've got cancer"? What do you say to your friends? We were struggling to come to terms with the news ourselves without having to worry about how other people might react. There was no easy way. So we adopted the direct way.

Reactions varied little. Mostly there was the initial shock that expressed itself as wide-eyed silence. Then came questions and occasionally tears, followed by sympathy and overwhelming offers of help. Everyone wanted to be there for Andrea, to take her to hospital appointments, to look after the kids, to make meals, wash and iron, take her out, do the shopping, anything. When your back's against the wall you know who your friends are. We found we had lots of friends.

And there was plenty of concern for me, too. "How are you coping, Matt?" "Are you OK, Matt?" I wasn't sure. I was on automatic pilot.

I wondered how Andrea was sleeping at night? (Badly, I think). I would lie beside her, my mind racing, full of 'ifs' and 'whens', yet there she lay, outwardly relaxed. There were a few evenings when the conversation turned to "Why me?" but on the whole she appeared to be doing remarkably well.

I was beginning to see myself as a navigator and buoyancy aid. I had to listen hard to everything said by the medical staff, understand it all, and steer Andrea through the minefield. And I had to boost her spirits, keep her fed and watered, strong and afloat.

Waiting for the day of the surgery felt like being tied to a train track, all the while hearing the rumbling of the express getting louder and louder. There was no escape, no putting it off until later. Andrea was holding herself together remarkably well. Mostly our discussions related to practical matters – childcare arrangements, re-arranging appointments – and on the whole she was displaying a positive attitude. There were moments when, emotionally, things threatened to fall apart like a house of cards in a hurricane, but in general it was business as usual. Andrea must have been like a swan on a fast flowing river – looking smooth and unruffled on the surface, but underneath kicking like crazy.

To allow us some relaxation and relief from the stress, Ann arranged to look after Hannah and William on the Saturday night following Andrea's diagnosis. We went to visit Mal and Andrea. An evening of worry-free adult company, with the odd drink or two, was a very welcome release. After a couple of bottles of wine the collarbone and cancer conversations didn't seem quite so depressing.

***

One thing that was important to us was to try and keep things as normal as possible – work, children, routines of relaxing and running – but normal was going to need re-defining.

By Monday my tummy bug had cleared, and I tried to fit in some quality training while I could, running four fast miles on two consecutive lunchtimes. Annoyingly, this caused minor pain to my right Achilles tendon area, something I had experienced before on the left side prior to the coast-to-coast. I knew this needed nipping in the bud, as healing of an Achilles problem can be very slow. I began icing it regularly and resting. In addition, Achilles strengthening exercises were added to the stretching routine I performed every morning upon waking. Some swimming and gym work was scheduled instead of running.

At work I scanned my Achilles using the ultrasound machine that I operate. There was a small area in the lower tendon where the fibres looked irregular and inflamed. This wasn't a serious injury but an annoyance that required careful handling. I figured that it would get sufficient rest when Andrea was recovering from her surgery.

***

Friday 8th December 2006

The day of the surgery arrived, and started conventionally – being woken at an ungodly hour by the kids, then a family breakfast after battling to get clothes on to wriggling infants. Everything was as usual except for the three overnight bags stationed by the front door. One of them was Andrea's with pyjamas, a wash kit and some trashy magazine. The other two contained clothes and overnight essentials for Hannah and William.

Hannah was going to school as normal as my sister, Kate, had kindly offered to pick her up afterwards and take her back to her house in Macclesfield for the weekend. Hannah fully understood the arrangements and was enthusiastically looking forward to seeing her cousins, Ella and Joe. William was on his way to Ann's for the weekend, after first spending time with my mother, June, who was helping out with the morning school run. Andrea had difficult goodbyes with the children, trying hard to keep her emotions contained.

The journey to the hospital was one we had both made thousands of times, but this time it was as patients rather than staff. We would experience life on the other side of the fence. I parked the car in the staff car park and we walked the hundred yards or so into the building alongside the newly-arriving day shift. The harsh buzzing of the intercom system announced our arrival at St. Mary's Ward, and we waited in silence to be admitted.

A short corridor led to a central nurses' station, the focal point for several patient rooms. Andrea was checked-in, and a nurse led her to an empty bed in a six-patient bay. I followed a few feet behind like a lost puppy, tightly gripping her bag in my right fist, as if holding on to it somehow symbolised holding on to her. She calmly arranged her things around the bed before drawing the curtains and changing into the gown provided by the nurse. I sat on the chair beside the bed, still feeling lost.

The hush in the room was broken by the clatter of teacups on top of a breakfast trolley being pushed along by a healthcare assistant. The only other sounds were the persistent ring of the telephone on the nurses' station, and the occasional electronic beep from distant medical equipment. I felt out of place and self-conscious in there, almost fearful, yet I was the one who could have walked out at any time. Andrea was the one being brave.

She re-appeared from behind the curtains and sat on the bed, looking a little awkward and semi-exposed in the cotton gown. We chatted - not much, but we chatted. What to say? Small talk seemed crass. Discussing the procedure, diagnosis, prognosis, and treatment seemed insensitive. So - we chatted about running and the Bolsover 10K which was only nine days away. It seemed out of the question that Andrea would be able to run, and she felt that all her training and preparation would be wasted. She had put in hundreds of miles, battled through storms and hot sun, and stuck to her program only to have another 'significant event' stop her in her tracks. So much for 'third time lucky'!. This time her training was being curtailed for a negative rather than a positive reason. She was bitterly disappointed, but I pointed out that the efforts had been far from wasted as she had dramatically increased her level of fitness. That had put her in a stronger physical position to battle through any treatment that might be necessary.

We sat for just a few minutes before the anaesthetist arrived. He explained in a clear and pleasant manner what would happen. As far as he was concerned there was absolutely nothing to worry about. Andrea was fit and well and would easily tolerate the anaesthetic. There were some consent forms to sign, after which he said he'd see her shortly, and left.

A few minutes later Mr Holt arrived. He sat on the bed next to Andrea, put his arm around her, and asked in a sincere manner how she was feeling. Such familiarity was not something that he would engage in with all his patients, but the two had known each other for many years. He explained again what was going to happen, and checked that Andrea understood before pulling the curtains around the bed for a final examination. He drew lines on the skin with a marker pen as a guide for the surgery, and hugged her one more time before moving off to the operating suites

We sat.

An uneasy quiet ensued, punctuated by comments about articles in the magazines we were both trying – but signally failing - to read. Thankfully it wasn't long before a porter arrived, accompanied by the nurse we saw earlier. The time had come for Andrea to go to theatre.

Relatives are usually required to leave at this point; however, as I was 'staff' I was allowed to accompany them down to the entrance to the operating theatre. Andrea lay there while the porter pulled the bed from the front, the nurse assisted from the back, and I walked in a daze alongside.

We headed down the main corridors and past the entrance to the Imaging Department where we both worked. I was choking up and hoped that nobody I knew would see us and come to talk. I don't think I could have spoken to anybody. Andrea must have felt worse - conspicuous and self-conscious being transported on a bed, wearing a hospital gown, and terrified at the prospect of what lay ahead. But she was brave. Bravery isn't about not being scared; that's foolishness. Bravery is about carrying on even though you are terrified.

Thankfully the two-minute journey to the theatre was uneventful. I went with her as far as I was allowed, and the nurse and porter stood back while we hugged and kissed. In a broken and croaky voice I told her how much I loved her, wished her good luck, and said I'd see her soon. She smiled as she was wheeled within and the doors swung quietly shut behind her.

Silence.

I was left staring into space, feeling completely helpless. Not that I could have done anything. I wasn't able to take the cancer away. I couldn't cast a spell and destroy the tumour. But at least I was there to support, to listen, to try and understand. Now I could do nothing more - except hope.

I was choking back the tears as I walked out of the hospital and to the car, still desperate to avoid anyone I knew. I needed distraction, so I drove into town and tried to busy myself with Christmas shopping. All the shops were festively decorated, all playing the usual seasonal songs we've heard a thousand times before. Market stalls sold roasted chestnuts, wrapping paper, tinsel and Santa hats. People bustled and jostled, and filled the steamy-windowed café's with their festive purchases and light-hearted chatter. The Salvation Army band *decked the halls with boughs of holly*. But overhead the sky was grey and flat, and so was I.

An all-day full-English breakfast and a cup of tea in a café tried its best to lift my spirits. But the first semblance of a smile was conspicuously absent until I telephoned St. Mary's Ward just after lunchtime to see if there was any news. I was told that Andrea was out of the operating theatre, and awake, the operation had gone smoothly, and that I could go and see her. I slurped down the last dregs of tea, and started jogging back to the car. The jog soon turned into a walk. Full-English breakfasts do not jog.

***

The first thing I did before heading back to the hospital was to telephone the relatives. I reported that the surgery had apparently gone well, and that Andrea was recovering nicely. Ann was extremely relieved to hear the positive news, and planned to call in to see Andrea herself on her way to pick William up from June. She had been driving herself wild with worry, and was looking forward to having her grandson with her to keep her distracted.

I managed to park in almost the same space I'd used earlier, and retraced my steps back to the ward, dizzy with nervousness, fear and anticipation. What was I going to find? How would Andrea be? Had they been able to remove the entire tumour? Was it all over?

What if they hadn't got it all out? What if Mr Holt had found something else? My mind was still whirling like a fairground ride as I pressed the ward intercom buzzer once more and waited to be let in. I strode back up the short corridor, turned left at the busy station, and into Andrea's bay.

She lay propped up on two pillows, awake but looking tired and uncomfortable. She was understandably very washed-out, and I didn't trouble her much with conversation. Once again I was totally useless. The best I could do was to sit and hold her hand. The telephone still rang on the nurses' station, distant medical equipment still beeped, and the teacups still rattled in another room. I sat, just looking, as time ticked away in an uncomfortable manner, oblivious to my surroundings.

I was preparing to leave when Mr Holt arrived. He wore the smile and manner of someone who was happy with recent events. He went on to explain that as far as he could tell the tumour had been completely removed, along with a number of lymph nodes, and he had encountered nothing unexpected. Surely this was great news? The tumour was out.

The removed tissues would be sent to the pathology laboratory for analysis. This was important to see what type the cancer was and whether it had started to spread to surrounding tissues. We were given an appointment to see him in his clinic a few days later to discuss further management.

A weak, December sun was setting over the hills to the west of Chesterfield as I ambled back to the car. I arrived home in semi darkness, without remembering any details of the five-mile drive through the centre of town. My mind had switched back to autopilot to get me home.

I didn't sleep very well that night. Saturday morning dawned cold and damp, and the bed gaped emptily without Andrea in it. I had woken on her pillow; the scent had drawn me to it as I slept. For a few moments I had forgotten she wasn't there. The house sounded normal; the central heating pump hummed, the bedroom clock ticked. Then the realisation thumped me in my stomach like a heavyweight boxer. The usual signs were absent. No warmth radiated from a slumbering body beside me. No feeling that the children would wake up at any moment and shout out to us. The house was an empty shell.

I stretched and showered quietly, lonely. This was the kind of undisturbed waking that I had regularly longed for through the tiring, child-filled, sleep-deprived nights that happened almost constantly. It was all a strain but I missed it. I wanted the family back.

Breakfast was neither full nor English. A cup of coffee and a croissant raised the blood sugar and caffeine levels sufficiently for me to get in the car and drive back to the hospital.

Andrea had just nibbled a small amount of her breakfast when I arrived, and was still propped up on her pillows with the adjustable small table positioned a few inches above her knees. She was feeling tired, sore and a little groggy, but was keen to go home. We had to wait for a doctor to come and assess her before she could be discharged. In preparation she had optimistically put on her own clothes and packed her night things back in the bag.

We didn't have to wait long. Mr Holt arrived and the curtains were drawn around the bed. I could see nothing but could hear clearly as he asked how she felt. She said she was fine, a little sore and tired but that was all. There had been no sickness following the anaesthetic, and she had managed to sleep in spells throughout the night. Importantly she had been able to eat and drink normally. These were good signs.

Andrea was discharged with the instruction to take it easy for a few days. Not surprisingly, she didn't feel like doing anything else. But she was still thinking about the Bolsover run, and before Mr Holt left she asked him what was the possibility of her making the race. He thought for a minute, and then said, "That's eight days away. It's *possible*." The emphasis on the merely *possible* made it sound to us like *unlikely*, but there was hope.

The walk to the car was a slow one as was the drive home. She walked carefully into the house and lay down, gently, on the sofa. The rest of the day was spent drifting in and out of sleep with me trying to help and not be a nuisance. I'm not sure I succeeded on either score.

However, I *did* become proficient at answering the phone before two rings had sounded. All our friends and family wanted to know how she was doing, and all wanted to come and visit. It was just like when we had returned home from hospital with the newborn children, but the atmosphere was naturally more sombre.

By early evening Andrea had perked up, and suddenly announced that she wanted a Chinese take-away. And it couldn't wait until I'd finished watching the football results on TV. Her wish was my command. In fact, her wish was my pleasure. I asked how she felt and was told to stop fussing. The Great Hunter went off and returned with sweet and sour chicken, boiled rice and vegetable chow mein. Andrea devoured it like she hadn't eaten for weeks.

Before heading for bed she took a bath, being careful not to wet the dressings under her right arm. After swallowing some of the prescribed painkillers, she propped herself up with pillows to get comfortable, and hoped the soreness would abate long enough for her finally to get a good night's sleep.

***

Hannah returned home on Sunday to find her mother uncomfortable but cheerful. William stayed with Ann for another night; he wasn't old enough to know not to jump on mum. The recovery was going well, so I returned to work on Monday morning. I had to save my holiday time in case I needed to be off work later.

The rest of the week was hectic. I had to take Hannah to school, and William to nursery, before heading to work. Running wasn't completely impossible, however, as I squeezed in a couple of short sprints on Tuesday and Wednesday. Thankfully my tendon seemed fine; I hoped I'd managed to sort *that* problem before it had become significant.

The Bolsover 10K was looming ever nearer, but the Gods seemed determined we wouldn't be there. Both children had kept us awake for several nights as they had caught bad colds. Then, the day before the race, Andrea succumbed to the same virus. With ridiculous optimism we took the children to Ann's the evening before the event, and tried to rest and prepare. Andrea hadn't run since before the surgery, and her wound was still very tender.

Race morning dawned and Andrea was definitely unable to compete. Her scar was increasingly painful and looked red and angry. This needed checking out as a wound infection was a possible complication. She telephoned the hospital and was told to go straight there. With our running clothes in a bag in the car, we set off immediately. If we were out of the hospital in time, our plan was for Andrea to drop me in Bolsover so that I could run the race alone before jogging the seven further miles from there to Ann's to meet the family.

The doctor was very quick examining the wound - there was no sign of infection, he said, but maybe Andrea's arm movements had inflamed the healing tissues – but he was not quick enough. By the time we left there were just ten minutes to the start of the race. But this no longer troubled us. On the current scale of anxieties it didn't even register. Although Andrea had worked hard for the event, she faced reality and resolved to run the race another time.

One day.

What *was* annoying, and rubbed salt into our metaphorical wound, was that we had to drive through Bolsover to get to Ann's. At the far end of town we had to stop to allow a stream of racers to pass in front of us. Looking at the pace they were moving, Andrea and I would probably have been among that bunch.

The running gods were being cruel that day!

***

Fight

Donna Ashley greeted us cheerfully and escorted us back into the smart consulting room, which looked exactly the same as it did previously. The furniture looked the same, the light through the window was the same, and the bushes outside had spectacularly failed to climb any higher up the fence. Even the atmosphere appeared similar. This worried me. The tumour was out. Mr Holt had said so himself. There should have been a mood of relief, but for some reason doubts and fears still gnawed away like an old dog with a favourite bone.

Mr Holt was waiting for us. Andrea's case notes were on the smart new desk in front of him. He began straightaway; no wasted unnecessary small talk that never helps anyway. His manner was as impeccable as before. The histology results were back! They were "OK". "Not perfect, but OK".

Out of the seventeen lymph nodes that had been removed at surgery, one tested positive for spread of the cancer. Just one! One measly, lousy, tiny, biological filter: the one nearest the tumour. Just one! But one was all it took.

One positive node meant that the cancer had started to spread from the primary tumour and had begun wandering around Andrea's body. Normal nodes would be comparable to having uprooted a dandelion weed in the garden whilst it was still a yellow flower. 'Node positive' was like having pulled up the dandelion only to find it had gone to seed, and some of the seeds may have blown off and been spread by the winds. A new weed could sprout up somewhere else!

One node positive; the seeds had started to spread. Was just one seed caught in that first lymph gland, meaning the entire cancer *had* been removed after all? Or were there more seeds circulating, waiting, lurking, about to start a new tumour somewhere else? It was impossible to know.

One positive node. That changed everything. There was a risk that cancer cells were still present. They had to be killed. Poisoned.

Andrea would have to undergo chemotherapy and quite likely radiotherapy after that. A specialist oncologist would oversee her treatment from now on. The first battle was over, but the war had hardly begun. It wouldn't be a short war. And it certainly wouldn't be all over by Christmas.

***

The first task was to get the cancer 'staged'. This meant getting a measure of how much it had grown and spread in order to decide on the best treatment and give an indication as to the prognosis. Cancers generally go through three stages – local growth and damage to nearby tissues, spread into lymph nodes, and then spread to other organs or areas of the body.

The 'TNM scale' is commonly used for staging purposes, and the lower the TNM values the better the outcome. TNM stands for 'Tumour', 'Nodes' and 'Metastases'. The tumour is assessed for its size and growth locally. Nodes refers to the number of lymph nodes affected, and their distance from the tumour, whilst metastases refers to the presence, or otherwise, of secondary tumours in other organs.

Andrea's tumour had not grown to involve tissues outside the breast, so it was T1. There was a single positive lymph node, so the N value was also 1. Whether any metastases had developed needed to be assessed to determine the M value.

In addition to staging, some cancers are also graded into low, intermediate or high (1,2, or 3) grade tumours, which is done by assessing the cells under a microscope. Low-grade tumours tend to be slower growing and less aggressive. High-grade tumours grow quickly and aggressively.

To stage Andrea's cancer it was necessary for her to have a

radioisotope bone scan, a chest X-ray, and an ultrasound scan of her liver. Bones, lungs and the liver are the likely sites to which breast cancer tends to spread, or 'metastasise'.

Another enthusiastic and helpful breast nurse, Helen Scott, had request cards for the examinations in her hand. Whilst Mr Holt examined Andrea's breast and surgical wound, I walked with Helen` down the short corridor to the Medical Physics department. The bone scan was arranged for the following day. The other tests would be done on the same visit.

I was at work the following day, and by chance was assigned to work in the Medical Physics Department's radiopharmacy, where the radioactive injections for the bone scans are made. With a colleague we removed some radioactive liquid from a special generator, and added it to a vial containing a dried phosphate substance. The radioactive liquid phosphate produced was then drawn into syringes to be injected into each patient having a bone scan that day.

When Andrea arrived for her tests, the Senior Chief Technician, Barry Parker, gave the injection into one of her arm veins. Andrea had to wait for two hours while the phosphate was taken up into her bones, after which time a scanner called a gamma camera was used to produce images of Andrea's skeleton.

The uptake of the phosphate in normal bones would be evenly distributed. Metastases would take up a higher amount of the phosphate, and with it more of the radioactivity. A normal looking skeleton would appear nice and even on the image. Any bright areas, or 'hot spots', would indicate metastases.

During the two-hour wait Andrea visited the X-ray department to have her chest X-ray. All the scan and X-ray pictures are stored digitally on a computer system, enabling them to be viewed on workstations around the hospital.

The chest X-ray was reported as clear – no metastases were present in the lungs.

My afternoon at work was spent in the ultrasound department. I had access to an imaging workstation. Curiosity got the better of me and I called up Andrea's bone scan images on the screen. Although no longer operating a gamma camera as part of my routine work I had spent several years doing so. I knew what a bone scan should look like.

The first thing to strike me was that there were extra pictures of Andrea's skull. Why had Barry taken extra pictures? I looked harder, and there was an unusual radioisotope uptake pattern near the top of her head. Barry had obviously seen this and decided he needed to investigate further. My head fell into my hands. I could feel my heart thumping harder in my chest. Bone metastases. Did this mean bone metastases?

I shouldn't have looked at the pictures. Trying to put what I had seen to the back of my mind and carry on with the afternoon's work proved very difficult. As soon as I had the opportunity I ran round to see Andrea in her office in the breast unit. She was calm, and told me that when the scan was finished she had been taken to see the Consultant Radiologist who was going to report it. The Radiologist, Dr Meiring, had looked at the pictures, and then looked harder at the extra skull images before turning to Andrea and announcing, "Normal."

There were no signs of bone metastases. The unusual appearance in the skull was symmetrical and didn't represent an abnormality. My relief must have been palpable, as Andrea looked at me in a bemused manner and asked, "What…?"

I told her I had seen extra pictures, and was terrified that something was wrong. She explained that Barry had thought the scan was normal but wanted to be sure, so he took more pictures. It felt like a giant hand had reached down and plucked me, gasping, from the bottom of a deep, water-filled pit in which I had been suffocating. I inhaled deeply with relief, and then returned back to work, feeling somewhat stupid.

A short while later I felt the need to have another look at the pictures. This time I could see that the uptake was symmetrical – exactly the same on both sides of her skull. No metastases. With hindsight, had I looked at an identical scan of a person unknown to me I would have considered it normal. Instead I had panicked and jumped to the wrong conclusion. Curiosity had nearly killed my cat. I needed to keep a clear head.

Later that day Dr Glaves performed the liver ultrasound examination. The test took just a few minutes, at the end of which he was able to reassure Andrea that there was no evidence of metastases in the liver either.

No metastases in the lungs, bones or liver. At last, some good news. The M value for staging was zero. The day had been traumatic due to my own impetuousness. Andrea took it all in her stride, but it was over, and the staging results were promising.

The cancer troubles were forgotten for Christmas Day, or at least not mentioned. The day was good, a family get-together at Ann's. We had a great meal and fun watching the children opening their presents. It was a nice way to end what had become a year of mixed but worsening fortunes. 2007 looked like it was going to be challenging in many ways.

The first challenge was unexpected. Every job at the hospital where Andrea and I worked was assessed in a 'Workforce Review'. The review decided that Andrea's post was unnecessary, and her job was 'disestablished'. The rug had been pulled from under her feet. She could continue with her work for a few months while she was offered, or found, an alternative post. If nothing suitable came up, she would be out of work. There is never a good time to receive news like this, but the timing couldn't have been worse.

***

Thursday 28th December 2006.

We made our way back to the hospital, this time to consult with the Oncologist to discuss the cancer, the best treatment, and all associated health and logistical issues. The Consultant's Registrar, Dr Perreira, first saw us.

Andrea and I sat beside his desk while he peered through wide spectacles in a thoughtful manner at her case-notes, mumbling things to himself. We kept quiet, occasionally glancing at each other instead.

Once he had all the facts sorted in his mind he started to speak, beginning with a quiet hum that rapidly increased to a growl.

"So, you have breast cancer.................on the right side................that has been removed.................but there was one positive lymph node...................."

He spun his head and looked over his glasses at us, turning his statement of fact into a question.

"Yes, that's right", replied Andrea.

"So, the treatment for your cancer will be chemotherapy, six cycles using a regime called FEC-T."

"OK," we both replied, and the question-and-answer session began in earnest.

Andrea, rightly, wanted to know everything – what the drugs were, the likely side effects, how long it would all take, how she would feel, and the most important issue – would she make a full and permanent recovery?

The last question was the hardest to answer. There *was* no answer. There were just statistics and probabilities, and every factor that was introduced to the theoretical equation confused the figures still further. It went something like this:

Out of a thousand women in exactly the same position, a certain number would have recurrence of the cancer within five years. A few more would have recurrence by ten years. Some others would get it again later than that. There are survival rates for five years and also for ten years. But all the numbers mean nothing on an individual level.

Imagine being in a crowd of a thousand people and having someone outside the crowd randomly firing a gun into the throng. Some people get shot. Some don't. It might be you, but it probably wouldn't be. How would you feel? Statistics and probabilities are all very well, but you either get shot or you don't.

The consultant oncologist was called Dr Purohit, a very forthright but pleasant man with a voice that was smooth yet raspy, rather like honey poured over gravel. He was very thorough and patient. He too read

Andrea's case-notes, and repeated many of the same statement-cum-questions as had Dr Perreira. He also gave us the same information, re-affirming the fact that chemotherapy was definitely required, as was radiotherapy.

He also added that further cellular analysis would be made on the removed tumour to find out the hormonal status of the cancer - whether it was oestrogen receptive or herceptin receptive – as this would also influence future treatment. The analysis so far indicated that the tumour was a high-grade, aggressive type. So the staging was T1N1M0, grade 2/3.

When the questioning was over, he asked Andrea to remove her T-shirt, he drew the curtains around the couch, and examined Andrea's breast and scar. He was quite happy with what he saw; however the chemotherapy couldn't begin until the scar had thoroughly healed. Before we left, the dates for treatment were arranged. The first session of chemotherapy was booked for Thursday January 25th.

We went home and wrote all the appointment dates in a diary – all the days when the chemotherapy would be administered, spaced three weeks apart, and then the predicted start date of the radiotherapy. From this we calculated the anticipated treatment finishing date. If - and it was a big if - everything went to plan and each treatment was administered on time, then it would be all over by late July. If any problems were encountered, and the nature of chemotherapy is such that problems are not uncommon, then it could extend into August.

This ruled out entering the Lyke Wake race on Saturday 7th July. But this didn't mean that running the route was impossible; I'd just have to arrange a date for a solo effort after the radiotherapy had been completed. That wasn't a problem. The problem would be training for an ultra-distance run when opportunities to run would be limited, and following a sensible training program would be almost impossible.

Running when Andrea was ill and suffering seemed somehow selfish. She would be stuck in the house, feeling terrible, and I could be out in the fresh air, exercising and enjoying myself. But my running benefited us both. It was an invaluable discharge from the stressful situation, liberation from the extra workload required to keep our ship afloat; it kept me fresh and energised, in a good mood and mentally buoyant. It also got me out from under Andrea's feet where I may have tended to fuss around her too much, and she got some well-deserved peace. So running actually took on a greater importance than it previously had. It had become a necessary release.

***

For the first couple of weeks in January my training had been ticking over rather than steadily progressing. Long runs were consistently stuck at around ten miles in distance. This was maintaining a solid base on which to build, still hopeful of being able to attempt the Lyke Wake, but it would have to be significantly increased if I retained serious hopes of running the 43-mile distance without an awful lot of pain. However, most of my long runs were off-road, and some of them were very hilly, which was better training than pottering around the pavements.

On the Saturday before Andrea's first dose of chemotherapy I ran a ten-mile loop through the local woods and up the valley around Linacre Reservoirs. I was wearing a backpack, and getting used to carrying gear that would be essential for the Lyke Wake. The weather was very windy, but sunny, and the trails were very wet and slippery. The run felt fantastic. I enjoyed every minute, feeling the freedom, pulling in vast lungfuls of fresh air, and being part of the natural world. I was only too aware that this may well be the last good run for quite some time, and made every effort to feel it and enjoy it.

I returned home just before sunset, covered in mud and sweat, and looking forward to an evening relaxing with Andrea in front of the television. Once again, fate decided that would be far too easy for us. William, now just over one year old, began vomiting shortly after we put him to bed. He continued to be ill all night - another night with no sleep.

Unable to keep any fluids down, he became dehydrated and very poorly. On Monday he needed hospital treatment. Andrea took him to the Children's Unit within the hospital, and a saline drip was connected into one of the veins in his arm to try to get fluids back into him. He was given a bed in a side-room where he had to stay overnight. Andrea stayed with him.

The next morning William was showing some signs of recovery, and had managed a few sips of water. At lunchtime Andrea rang me at work to say he had been discharged and they were back at home. But when I arrived home that evening he had begun to be sick again, and was as poorly as the previous day. He had been discharged too early.

After consulting the doctors on the paediatric unit we were told to take him back. Andrea hadn't slept for two nights, so I took William, along with an overnight bag for me. With only three days to go before starting chemotherapy, Andrea needed to be as fit, strong and rested as she could be. Sleep was essential.

Once again, a saline drip needed inserting into his arm. This proved to be a difficult and traumatic experience for all concerned. Thirteen-month-old babies don't have big veins in which to stick needles easily, and the ones William did have had been battered by trying to get the line in the day before. He screamed and wriggled; I fought to hold him still, and the flustered doctor sweated, toiled, and constantly apologised for her failed efforts.

Eventually a thin pipe was inserted, enabling fluids to pass slowly into his tiny veins from a bag suspended above his head and through a machine that measured the flow rate. But the line had a tenuous grip on its function. If William moved his arm then the line blocked. Every time the pipe blocked the machine sounded an alarm and had to be reset.

As William lay there, he was in a world somewhere between awake and asleep, distressed but not crying. His weakened body was buried in his baby-grow, and his sunken eyes ever so slightly open as if he were squinting at something. I sat on the other bed at the edge of the small room, and watched the drip machine, seeing the numbers on the display rise if he held his arm still, but fall when he moved, resulting in the alarm sounding.

When this happened a nurse came in the room to reset the device but it was taking longer each time for her to arrive. The staff were so busy as the children's ward was completely full, mostly with babies in a similar state to William. I took to standing by the cot, holding his arm still to help maintain the flow of fluid, but this was tough. He was very uncomfortable and restless, and constantly moved and rolled around the cot. As the night drew on, holding his arm proved more and more difficult, and I was getting increasingly tired. The ward was in darkness, and in the small hours of the morning exhaustion crept over me, and I crept over to the bed, hoping William had finally gone to sleep himself.

I didn't bother to undress; I just lay down and pulled a sheet over myself. I could only have been asleep for half an hour before a nurse entered the room to record William's temperature and check the drip machine. I felt surprisingly self-conscious lying on the bed next to William's cot, and forced myself to sit up and watch proceedings despite being unable to help in any way. As the nurse left the room I lay back down and hoped for a few hours sleep.

***

"Would you like some breakfast?"

I woke with a start, unable to work out where I was for a few seconds.

"Oh, er, yes please. What have you got?" I replied.

The healthcare assistant left me two slices of toast and a cup of tea before rattling her trolley round to the next side-room. As I enjoyed the food, I peered over at William, who was in much the same position as I had left him in the small hours of the morning. The bag of fluid was almost empty.

"This must be a good thing," I thought, "His hydration level must have improved". Somehow he looked better, pinker, and more normal than he had before I grabbed the short sleep.

The drip finally finished, and was removed, although the cannula needle was left in his arm in case it was needed again. At nine o'clock in the morning the paediatric doctor came to review William. He was pleased with his progress, and sure enough, William was starting to sit up in bed and wanted to play. The decision was made that if he could drink two beakers of water and not be sick, and if his nappy was getting wet, proving his kidneys were working, then he could go home.

With one false discharge already we were keen to be sure he really was well before I took him home. By lunchtime we were in the car making the all too familiar drive from the hospital back home.

Andrea was delighted to see him smiling at her as I carried him through the door. Thankfully she had managed to sleep well, and William's troubles had taken her mind off her own impending medical onslaught.

But we just couldn't believe our bad luck. How much sickness was coming our way? I began to feel like Coleridge's *Ancient Mariner* after having killed the albatross.

***

Chemo

Andrea was to undergo six cycles of chemotherapy, spaced three week apart. Each cycle was intended to poison and destroy any cancer cells. But the drugs would also poison her healthy cells, with numerous and extremely unpleasant effects.

After each cycle she would have a few days to recover before having to endure it all again.

And again!

And again, until she had been chemically pounded and tortured six times.

FEC-T chemotherapy is a treatment regime combining four different cytotoxic (cell killing) drugs. The first three are given in combination for the first three cycles. The initial letter of each – Fluorouracil, Epirubicin and Cyclophosphamide – make up the 'FEC' part of the treatment name. The 'T' is from Taxotere (also known as Docetaxel) which is the fourth cytotoxic drug given, and is given alone for the last three cycles.

Fluorouracil is one of the most common cancer treating drugs, and is an 'anti-metabolite'. These are molecules that are slightly different to ones normally found within the body. The differences cause them to stop cells making and repairing DNA, which is the genetic code within the nucleus that controls their multiplication. This is how they prevent cancer cells growing and multiplying, but they also do it to normal cells.

Epirubicin binds to the DNA of cancer cells, causing it to tangle and be unable to reproduce. Again this also happens to normal healthy cells.

Cyclophosphamide sticks to DNA, preventing cell division. And guess what? This too binds to healthy cell DNA.

The chemotherapy would be indiscriminate – the napalm strike of medicine. Any cell trying to reproduce would be prevented from doing so. Cancer cells would try to replicate rapidly, and would hopefully be hit hardest by the cell-killing invasion. But there are plenty of other rapidly reproducing tissues in the body that would be destroyed in the collateral damage – blood cells, stomach lining, hair follicles, reproductive cells, skin, and more.

This is why chemotherapy causes a multitude of side effects. Commonly the unwanted effects of chemotherapy result from a drop in the number of blood cells. The reduction in blood cell numbers starts around the seventh day after treatment, and lasts for three to four weeks. The drop occurs due to impaired production of new cells in bone marow, and may result in infections and diminished immunity, tiredness and breathlessness, headaches, aching muscles, a cough, sore throat, pain whilst passing urine, flu-like symptoms, bruising more easily, nose bleeds, or bleeding gums after brushing teeth.

Some of these side effects can be life threatening.

Other potentially common side effects include nausea and vomiting, fatigue, complete hair loss, loss of appetite, diarrhoea, fluid retention, a metallic taste and a sore mouth, and loss of fertility.

To continue with the list of potential horrors of the chemotherapy treatment barely seems necessary. But I will.

Less commonly experienced may be skin changes including soreness, redness and peeling of the hands and feet, nail changes, irritated eyes, inflamed lungs, liver and kidney changes, damage to heart muscle leading to an irregular heartbeat, inflammation around the injection site, sensitivity of the skin to sunlight, allergic reactions, and numbness and tingling.

And if that still were not enough, in rare cases angina, heart failure or a heart attack may occur, there may be confusion and unsteadiness, and even another cancer can be caused in future years if high doses of the therapeutic drugs are used.

It really is quite charming stuff. But it's not entirely bad - looking on the humorous side, the urine could become a bright pink colour the day after having epirubicin. That, I wanted to see.

Andrea tried not to consider the potential side effects. She knew of two, and they were the two she feared most: nausea and hair loss. She wasn't good with sickness, and what woman would like losing her hair?

There was little that could be done to prepare for any nausea, but Andrea had a plan to try to minimise the impact of hair loss. One of her closest friends, Marie, is a hairdresser. Prior to beginning the treatment Andrea visited Marie, and had a dramatic re-styling. The flowing, blonde, shoulder-length locks were cropped into a short bob. I liked the bob. I thought she looked even more beautiful.

***

Thursday January 25th 2007

I escorted Andrea to the chemotherapy clinic within the Cavendish Suite situated a short way from where we both worked. The entrance opened into a small waiting area three quarters full with patients, all in various stages of their own chemotherapy conflict. Andrea gave her name to the receptionist who seemed to be guarding the short walk to the clinical rooms. I peered down out of curiosity, wondering what horrors lay beyond. The receptionist was the boatman Charon, I thought, who controlled our passage over the river Styx from Earth into Hades, the underworld.

The mythological Greek gods all respected the Styx and swore oaths by it. I swore anything I could think of for Andrea to be cured by the nurses and their concoctions down the corridor. Some stories say that the Styx had miraculous powers, and that it could make people immortal. How appropriate! I didn't hope for immortality for Andrea, just the restoration of her life to what it should be had this disease not struck her.

In mythology, the Styx circled the underworld nine times. I wondered how often *we* would have to make the journey.

Two things struck me. The first was that the waiting area was hot and stuffy, with too many people crammed into a small, badly ventilated space. The second was that the general atmosphere was far more upbeat and positive than one would expect with so many people waiting to 'pay the ferryman' and head down the corridor to be poisoned. Stoicism abounded. Positive mental attitudes shone like beacons of hope through what could otherwise have been the darkness of despair.

Several women of various ages sat chatting happily to each other across the small area, and their husbands and boyfriends regularly chipped in with the chat. Many of them had an unusual appearance, and initially I couldn't put my finger on what it was. Then it struck me. Eyebrows! They were mostly missing. Several wore headscarves on what were evidently heads devoid of any hair. A few looked normal, hair-wise, due to the excellent quality of their wigs. One confident lady proudly sported her bald head as though it were the trophy of a war she was fighting, and heading for victory.

Conversation revolved around the nuances of chemotherapy, blood results, and the sharing of tips to help cope with nausea, hair loss and infections. It was all very matter-of-fact, but also friendly, as if each woman had coped with the unpleasantness of having been stripped of part of what made her a woman in the first place, but was coming through the other side intact and willing to support others about to go through the same process. It was tragic, yet admirable and totally uplifting. Everyone was afflicted by the same disease, was fighting the same demon, and if they all stuck together, by God that enemy was going to stand no chance. Andrea and I were the new kids on the block, looking very green and frightened. She was terrified. She really, really didn't want to be there.

A nurse called for Andrea and we stepped forward. She directed us to the first side-room off the short corridor and we took our first steps onto the Styx. She introduced herself as Lydia, Andrea's chemotherapy nurse, and invited us to sit down.

She was a similar age to us and was even more calming than the ambience of the waiting room. She was nicely spoken, knowledgeable, helpful and sympathetic and recorded Andrea's height, weight and blood pressure. She then took a blood sample to send away for analysis to make sure there were sufficient blood cells for the chemotherapy to proceed.

Lydia went on to explain by what method the drugs would be administered, and in what order, stating that the first thing to be injected would be an anti-sickness agent.

She had been a chemotherapy nurse for some time and was able to describe the likely feelings and sensations that Andrea may experience during the treatment, explaining that while one of the drugs is injected it may produce the sensation of falling slowly backwards into nettles.

General health advice was given to try and help maintain good nutrition and a buoyant immune system, which included aiming for a diet full of fruit and vegetable 'super-foods', and dark chocolate. Plenty of dark chocolate. There may have been a huge, dark cloud overhead, but *there* was a glimpse of silver lining!

When all the advice and information had been carefully dispensed, Lydia asked if Andrea understood it, and how she was feeling. We both understood. Andrea was terrified and quite tearful. She had the look of a rabbit standing frozen in the headlights of an oncoming truck.

The blood results wouldn't be back until eleven o'clock. There was enough time to get some food and a drink so we wandered along to the hospital's staff canteen. I encouraged Andrea to eat what she could, as she might not feel like eating for some time after the treatment. The bacon and beans on toast wasn't the best we've ever had, but it was good enough, and the cup of tea was more than adequate. Andrea looked like she was struggling to eat hers, I suspect due to nerves, but she managed to force it all down eventually.

We sat staring out of the window, occasionally glancing at each other, holding hands and trying to think of things to say. We hoped the blood results would be abnormal so we didn't have to go through with it today, but at the same time we hoped the bloods were fine so we could get started with the treatment. We hoped it wouldn't be traumatic and painful. We hoped to be back home soon. We hoped the kids were OK. We hoped! Hope springs eternal.

Alexander Pope's poem, *An Essay on Man*, seemed highly appropriate. This work was an attempt to rationalise and use philosophy to "vindicate the ways of God to man"; Man cannot know God's purpose, so cannot complain about the things that befall him. *An Essay on Man* popularised optimistic philosophy after it was published in the eighteenth century. All four parts of the work are a thought-provoking read. Some snippets spoke volumes for us as we stared, and waited, and hoped.

> *Hope springs eternal in the human breast;*
> *Man never is, but always to be blest:*
> *The soul, uneasy and confin'd from home,*
> *Rests and expatiates in a life to come.*

> *He hangs between; in doubt to act, or rest;*
> *In doubt to deem himself a God, or Beast;*
> *In doubt his mind or body to prefer;*
> *Born but to die, and reas'ning but to err;*
> *Alike in ignorance, his reason such,*
> *Whether he thinks too little, or too much.*

We tried not to think too little or too much. Sitting in that canteen the time dragged laboriously, but also flew by too fast. Eleven o'clock slowly lumbered itself around all too quickly and we wandered back to the Cavendish Suite. Andrea checked back in with 'Charon', and re-seated herself amongst the stoics in the still hot and stuffy waiting room. Some fresh air would have been good. We would have felt much better if we'd been allowed to get out for a run. No running today though. Running had run out. Time had run out. Lydia called Andrea's name and we stood up. 'Charon' smiled and watched as we were led the few steps across the Styx and into Hades.

***

The suite was light and airy, and some extra brightness beamed from the winter sun as it crept tiredly above the southern horizon and shone timidly through the corner of the west-facing windows. Six or seven comfortable-looking armchairs were arranged around the edges of the room, each accompanied by a small, wheeled table and a drip stand, and all bar one occupied by patient receiving treatment. The husband or partner was sitting beside them, some talking, others reading newspapers. A few of the women were wearing what appeared to be a blue, padded crash helmet, giving them quite a comical appearance.

Lydia led Andrea through the room, past the other occupants who all smiled and said hello, to the vacant chair in the far left corner. I followed and stood uncomfortably, not knowing whether to stay or leave, until Lydia offered me the chair next to Andrea. From there I could see out of the window and down to the car park where our own car waited patiently to whisk us quickly home after the unknown ordeal was over.

Lydia took time to explain once again what would happen, and we both listened intently as before. We'd been joined by breast nurse Donna Ashley who had very kindly taken the time to sit with us through the first chemo session. Andrea was given the choice of whether to try a cooling cap. This was the strange-looking blue padded helmet, the purpose of which was to try and minimise hair loss. The cap, freezing cold, was designed to cool the scalp. This would, in theory, cause the blood vessels in the scalp to close up. The effect would be to reduce the blood flow delivered to the hair follicles and with it the amount of cell-killing drug. There was no guarantee it would work, but there was no harm in trying, other than getting a very cold head - and looking like a 1970's stuntman!

Lydia had to find a suitable vein in Andrea's arm for the needle. It had to be in the left arm as the surgery had removed lymph nodes from the right underarm area. The armchair had an electronic control panel enabling it to recline and the footrest to rise upwards, producing an almost horizontal position. Andrea was invited to experiment with the chair until she was comfortable as she would be in it for about an hour. She reclined a little, raised the feet a little, and sat there looking a lot less terrified than I would have been.

Lydia nipped away to get all the necessary equipment and drugs. We sat in silence. Donna calmed the tension with reassurances that the session would be less traumatic than expected, and that all the treatment would be over sooner than we thought. It was difficult to see light at the end of the tunnel. If there *was* any light it looked remarkably like the headlamp of a freight train thundering towards us at a hundred miles an hour.

Six months - that was a long time to be systematically poisoned, and then burned with radiation. We both wondered how six months of chemotherapy and radiotherapy could possibly be over sooner than we thought.

Lydia slid a tourniquet onto Andrea's left arm and pulled it tight. The first search for a vein began. There was some rubbing, some slapping, and general prodding and poking around the inside of Andrea's elbow and on the back of her hand. Finally a suitable vessel was chosen and, with only a quick wince from Andrea, the cannula was inserted. A small drip of blood flowed back through the tube confirming that it was suitably seated inside the vein. Access had been achieved; the route of invasion established. Three large syringes full of cell-killing drugs stood to attention on the tray next to Lydia.

A healthcare assistant arrived with the cooling cap. It was a tight fit; firm contact had to be made with the scalp to stand any chance of its being successful. This was hard to achieve and very uncomfortable for Andrea. There was a lot of pushing and straining, wiggling and twisting, and every movement appeared to tug painfully at her hair. I imagined it was going to wrench it from the roots rather than spare it from the chemical weapons.

Finally it was in place, and Andrea grimaced at the freezing effect. She was having an intense 'ice-cream-headache' – such as when you eat or drink something very cold too quickly, causing a sharp pain in your forehead. Not pleasant for her, but it looked funny to me, bringing a moment of light-hearted black humour to the proceedings.

Lydia called over one of the other chemo nurses, and together they checked Andrea's drugs, both of them reading out the names and the expiry dates on each syringe to ensure everything was correct. First to go in was an anti-sickness agent. In terms of volume this didn't amount to much – just a few millilitres. Then the syringe containing Fluouracil was lifted from the tray and attached to the end of the short line leading to the cannula.

Andrea slowly closed her eyes, and Lydia slowly squeezed the syringe.

***

Waves

Outwardly there was nothing different– Andrea chatted, and still grumbled about the ice-cream-headache. Donna chatted, I chatted, Lydia started to get to know about Andrea and our children, and we learned a bit about her. It was a perfectly normal social exchange between perfectly normal people. We could have been sitting having coffee together, or at a dinner party. All perfectly normal, but internally the cellular destruction had begun.

After a few minutes the Fluouracil syringe was fully discharged. Lydia unhitched it and loaded up the second, the Epirubicin. This was filled with rose-coloured fluid that gave the clear plastic line leading to the cannula a pleasing pink tinge as it was eased through.

Still nothing unusual happened. Andrea felt fine. By now it was lunch time, and I began munching on the cheese-salad baguette that I had bought on the walk back to the Cavendish Suite. Andrea also had a baguette, and slowly managed to nibble half of it as she sat partially reclined, under the blue helmet, and under attack. Nerves had scared hunger away, but she knew she needed to try and keep her strength up for the fight. Food was necessary. The chemo was necessary.

The cooling cap had slowly warmed to an ineffective temperature, and needed to be changed. A new blue crash helmet was carried from the freezer to replace the one that had been smothering Andrea's head. The head-wrestling routine was repeated, including the grimaces, the grunts and groans of a protracted struggle and a sub-zero scalp.

The pink potion was finished, and the third drug, Cyclophosphamide was loaded and ready to be injected. Two down, one to go! So far, so good! But we had been lulled into a false sense of security. Almost as soon as Lydia started pushing the plunger Andrea felt woozy. Her head spun with an alien dizziness, pins and needles pricked her skin, and the chair tried to suck her down into an unpleasant sickening blackness, like the bad symptoms of a drunken hangover with none of the pleasantness beforehand. Andrea asked for a sick bowl, and held it if front of her face expectantly, describing the feeling as if she had eaten something rancid and decomposing and was waiting for her body's violent rejection. But nothing happened. The feeling didn't ease. By the time the third syringe was empty she wore a slightly vacant expression, with her mouth and nose wrinkled as if subjected to a rotten, stale smell.

Lydia removed the needle from Andrea's arm, and congratulated her for having ploughed through the first treatment courageously. The cooling cap was removed jerkily, leaving Andrea with a bed-head hairstyle.

When she came to stand up from the chair the wooziness and nausea persisted. Strength and balance had been stripped from her legs. We thanked Lydia and Donna for their help and kind attention, and, offering Andrea an arm to hold for support, I escorted her slowly and deliberately back towards the car park. Andrea still carried the vomit bowl in her left hand.

As we exited the building the cold, crisp winter air plunged into her lungs and she stopped for a moment to pull in some slow, deep breaths. She looked like she was "away with the fairies", and the fairies had been spiking her drinks. For a moment I doubted she'd make it as far as the car, but then she leaned forwards and strolled purposefully onwards, inhaling heavily and blowing hard with every breath.

***

I drove into our driveway at around 2.30 in the afternoon and we walked slowly together into the house. Andrea was still feeling tired and light-headed, so she decided to go straight to bed. I left her snuggled but uncomfortable, and wandered back downstairs thinking to busy myself with chores.

The house seemed quiet and vacant, and I felt lost in it. Not that it was big; more that it was usually filled with noise, children, life and spirit, and all that seemed to have drained away into a strange disconcerting emptiness. I wasn't in control. I could do nothing to rid Andrea of the poison, and I didn't know how to look after her now. How do you help someone who is taking chemotherapy? I had no manual, no lessons, and couldn't even guess which of the countless side effects I'd have to ease Andrea through. I'd just have to wait and see what happened and make it up as I went along.

I didn't dare embark on any household job that I couldn't immediately stop to tend to Andrea, should she need it. As it happened she didn't need anything for hours; she just tried to sleep, hoping to sleep through any queasiness. But sleep didn't come. Andrea didn't 'do' sick. She hated feeling sick, despised being sick and even struggled in dealing with the children when they were sick. Sick was bad, very bad.

Hannah wondered where Mummy was when my mother brought her home after school. She didn't fully understand, but complied with my instructions to play downstairs and try to stay quiet. William knew something was amiss, and it was much harder keeping him from heading to Andrea for a cuddle.

In the early evening I convinced her to come downstairs and try to eat some of the meal I had just prepared. This was nothing fancy; something I thought she might be able to stomach - sausages, mashed potato and broccoli that I had cobbled together quickly for the children. They loved it, wolfing it down and asking for more. She tried to eat, but couldn't manage much.

While trying to keep one eye on Andrea I bathed the children and readied them for bed. They didn't get much of a story that evening, as I wanted to get back downstairs as soon as possible. Thankfully both children went to sleep quickly (although as usual William woke and cried out every few hours through the night).

Andrea's energy had completely drained away. Barely able to raise her head she lay on the sofa, staring at the television in an attempt to distract herself from the feeling that there were worms in her stomach, writhing, wriggling, swelling in size and sliding their way up the back of her throat before oozing back down into a horribly swirling gastric mass. Queasiness built steadily in intensity, washing over in waves; vicious tides of desire to vomit flooded her every sensation before retreating to the pit of her belly, only to rise up again a few minutes later.

Unable to take it anymore, Andrea sat up. But that didn't help. Tearful and moaning with her head in her hands, she rocked backward and forward with every surge of sickness. And all the while I was helpless, a mere spectator relegated to the basically fruitless tasks of rubbing her rocking back and muttering rambling phrases about how it was going to be alright and how she'd feel much better soon. But she didn't feel better soon. She felt much worse.

I only just managed to get the bowl under her chin a millisecond before the first vomiting started. Then, somehow, she managed to haul her poisoned nauseated body upstairs to the bathroom before violently bringing up the undigested baguette that she ate for lunch. The time was 9.30 at night, exactly eight hours after the chemotherapy treatment started. After twenty minutes of retching, coughing and vomiting she was completely empty, yet still in agony and still feeling sick. She was crying, and I was tearful at the helplessness of it all. All I could do was assist her into bed and cuddle her in a futile attempt to help her sleep.

The anti-sickness drugs had not been effective enough. We'd been given a whole array of medication designed to counteract some of the side effects, but some of this medication produced side effects of its own. And I needed a large piece of paper and a pen to work out exactly what tablets she should take at what time to be most effective. This was an organisational nightmare.

The list began with two anti-emetics (anti-sickness drugs), cyclizine and ondansetron. The cyclizine tablets had to be taken one at a time, three times a day, whilst the ondansetron was one tablet twice a day. On the paper I wrote down the time it would be best to have each, alternating and spacing them evenly. It was arranged so that the order was cyclizine, ondansetron, cyclizine, ondansetron, cyclizine. The timing had to fit in with when I anticipated Andrea first waking in the morning, and also going to sleep at night.

Then there were the steroids. Dexamethasone, a powerful corticosteroid, was prescribed to increase the effectiveness of the ondansetron. The dosage was one tablet four times a day. Some of the unwanted effects of dexamethasone include stomach upset, increased sensitivity to stomach acid, stomach ulcers, increased appetite leading to weight gain, reduced immunity, and possibly withdrawal problems.

As well as the anti-emetics and steroids, an antacid called omeprazole was required to counteract the unpleasant effects of a stomach wall stripped of new cell lining by the chemo, which would add to the sensitivity to stomach acid caused by the dexamethasone. The omeprazole was to be taken one capsule per day for two weeks after the chemo.

The times when the antacid and steroids should to be taken were added to the paper. The pill-popping program initially looked something like this:

7:00am cyclizine, dexamethasone, omeprazole
11:00am ondansetron
12:00pm dexamethasone
3:00pm cyclizine
5:00pm dexamethasone
7:00pm ondansetron
10:00pm cyclizine, dexamethasone

The nature of Andrea's symptoms made adhering to this complicated regime almost impossible. A side effect of the cyclizine is drowsiness. The chemo made her very tired. The result was that she was regularly drifting in and out of sleep, and was often dozing when she should have been taking drugs. Missed doses required a constant re-jigging of the program, frequently changing times and modifying the tablet intake to try to keep on top of the nausea.

To compound the problem further, some of the tablets should be taken with food. How do you do this if the patient can't eat? What started out as an A4 sheet of paper on which times and drugs were neatly written gradually evolved into a sheet full of scribbles, arrows and crossings out.

And then of course there was the vomiting. Any sickness would eject the recently swallowed medication, rendering it useless. This increased the likelihood of further bouts of sickness and the depressingly inevitable drift into a vicious circle of being sick because there were no anti-sickness drugs ingested, and not being able to ingest anti-sickness drugs due to being sick.

***

The children woke me the following morning. I tried to keep them quiet as Andrea was finally managing to doze, but they played, shouted and argued as I attempted to dress and feed them. At 7:00 am I carried a small pot containing one cyclizine, one dexamethasone and one omeprazole tablet into the bedroom to Andrea, along with a small glass of milk to help wash them down.

This was the start of the first proper attempt at the drug program. It began promisingly. Although waves of nausea regularly washed over her like an Atlantic swell, Andrea swallowed the pills and drank the milk, before drifting back to sleep. Ann arrived, took Hannah to school and William home with her. I now had only Andrea to look after for the weekend as Kate had offered once again to collect Hannah from school.

Andrea felt, and looked, completely washed-out all day. The cycles of queasiness continued unceasingly. She ate and drank very little, and slept a lot. The effectiveness of the anti-emetics was questionable, as she didn't manage to take the tablets on time. She was eventually sick, although not as violently as the night before.

We both went to bed early to try and catch up on lost sleep.

By Saturday the vomiting had stopped, but the queasiness hadn't. Andrea was still exhausted and sleeping a lot. The sickness and inactivity had left her feeling dirty and uncomfortable. I ran a bath, and helped her to undress and climb into the soothing, warm water. She had little strength to get in and out of the tub unaided, but felt much better for having cleaned the grime and filth from her body. It was as if she had washed away some kind of residue, some chemotherapy 'scum' that had coated her skin, suffocated her senses.

I helped her to dry and dress in clean clothes which provided a remarkable lift to the way she felt and looked. But the 'scum' still clung to the atmosphere of the house

The food intake still hadn't increased much by Sunday. When Andrea stood on the bathroom scales she found that she had lost seven pounds in three days. But she felt she was picking up, strength-wise. The anti-sickness drugs were being taken more often and at the appropriate times, and hunger was starting to return. By the evening she was eating again, and managed to stand in the shower and wash her hair. This brought back much needed feelings of femininity and confidence, and made her more able to cope with the imminent return of the children.

She was delighted when first Kate brought Hannah home, then Ann and Roy returned with William. She couldn't run around with the children, but her face lit up as William hugged her and Hannah spoke excitedly about the things she had been doing with her cousins. The chemotherapy rollercoaster appeared to be pulling out of the dip into which it had been plummeting since Thursday, and was heading back upwards towards sunshine and blue skies.

But the bounce-back proved to be short-lived. Monday morning dawned cold and damp and was matched in every respect by Andrea's general well-being. The tiredness had returned and, along with it the feeling of having been poisoned. she was being sick once again. This didn't seem right. The improvement had been obvious for all to see; yet now, four days after the chemo, she relapsed. As the day progressed there was little sign of improvement. Andrea rang the help number she had been given and spoke to experts at a local cancer centre in Sheffield.

The nurse at Weston Park Hospital advised her to go for a review and have her blood values checked. I needed to return to work, so my mother, June, kindly took Andrea and waited with her for the doctor. This took a long time as they didn't have a fixed appointment and Weston Park hospital is a bustling, busy place.

Unaware of the goings-on I'd taken the opportunity to get out for a quick lunchtime run. My body felt that I had done far too much sitting around over the last few days, and as soon as I completed the morning's work I bounded enthusiastically through the door and out into the winter's chill. The run wasn't scenic or long – a swift four-mile dash made up of laps around the hospital's perimeter road – but as a stress release it was wonderful. My feet pounded the tarmac and my arms pumped backward and forward as it they were punching that chemotherapy and beating that cancer into oblivion. Blood coursed through my veins like galloping racehorses while the cold air scoured any dust and debris from my lungs.

Meanwhile Andrea's blood was coursing into a syringe at another hospital before being put in a machine for analysis. I sprinted, Andrea waited; the blood analysis machine couldn't be hurried. When it eventually printed out the results, they were within normal range. The white cell count should be within the range of 4 – 10 (the unit of measurement escapes me). Andrea's read 5.8. There was no treatment to offer her other than advice to rest and to continue to look after herself as best she could.

***

Another day brought another change in the direction of the winds that were blowing chance and fortune through our lives, but this time for the better. Andrea was feeling some improvement, and eating again. Her strength steadily built up throughout the week. By Thursday she admitted to "feeling fine", and on Friday even considered herself "back to normal".

Indeed, a sense of normality was settling throughout the home, although this felt fragile. Meals were eaten, children entertained, and household chores were performed as they always had been, but we were still on our guard, constantly glancing over our shoulders and waiting for another bomb to drop.

I even dared to think about the Lyke Wake, and attempted a more structured exercise regime. This comprised an upper body workout on Tuesday evening, running a fast four miles on Wednesday, and then running again on Thursday; this time six hilly miles. Friday and Saturday were recovery days, time spent with the family

On Sunday I decided to take William out of Andrea's way for a while, give him some fresh air, and use him for some resistance training (in an attempt to replicate running up the hills of the North York moors). I ran wearing a backpack, and pushing him in his pushchair. The plan was to be out for a couple of hours, but William had other ideas. He was very grizzly and bad-tempered, and cried and whinged most of the time we were moving. I had to keep stopping to pacify him. We didn't get far, but it was better than nothing, and it gave Andrea a break.

The recovery from chemo was eventually going so well that, eleven days after the treatment, Andrea dared to go back to work. Things were still undecided regarding her job but she was happy trying to get back to normal. By evening her efforts had taken their toll; she was tired, but did manage to work again the following day. The fatigue was cumulative, however, and although she did her best to fight it, she was drained and run-down by the end of the third day of working.

Sore throat and flu-like symptoms invaded her abused body, and working on the Thursday wasn't an option. She was forced by fatigue to stay at home where she watched snow falling steadily outside, covering the ground with several inches of crisp, white beauty.

The snow was too tempting for me to ignore. I took opportunities to get out and run in it twice that day. I know many people would prefer to remain indoors, either to ignore the snow altogether or admire its aesthetic charm from the warmth of an armchair. But I love it.

I love the pleasing crunch under each footstep. I love the way it accentuates shadows and reflects light in ways you don't otherwise see. I love the manner in which it muffles and deadens any sound, giving the impression of isolation. And I love that it makes you work harder to run through it, requiring more energy, more balance and more concentration.

Traction when snow-running isn't usually a problem, as I tend to use trail shoes that have a more aggressive tread pattern than road-running shoes. If it's particularly slippery I wear fell-shoes. These have many soft rubber studs that stick a centimetre or so out from the sole. Slipping in them is almost impossible.

The five miles at lunchtime chilled my fingers and toes, leaving them glowing and red through the afternoon work session. Then in the evening I donned my weighted backpack, wore a head torch, and set off for a slow and steady but hugely enjoyable hour-long off-road run through Linacre Woods and around the reservoirs.

The normally black-brown and lifeless winter trees were white and sparkled like a fairy wedding. Boughs hung low, laden with the weight of a gazillion glittery flakes. Some of them draped themselves across the path, lying so low that I almost had to crawl under them. The trails I had run innumerable times became unrecognisable; the trees were different shapes, the ground all one colour and smoothed of all unevenness by the commanding wave of the snow queen.

The beam of my head torch reflected off the surface and cast dancing shadows in all directions as if tree sprites were leaping out to catch a glimpse of me before diving back under cover. My footsteps kicked the ice crystals upwards, exploding bombs of glitter in the light in front of my face. This was magical, like running through the back of the wardrobe and into Narnia. It was escapism *extraordinaire*. I didn't feel the cold; I just wandered through wonderland.

But the following morning I felt pain in my right foot, although I couldn't remember hurting it on the run, and pain in my throat. This developed into a minor cold that prevented me from running for several days, but at the same time it provided the opportunity for my foot trouble to settle. The minor cold was probably the same thing that had slowed Andrea's recovery; with her newly reduced immunity it had hit her much harder than me.

A few days of resting helped us both immensely, and Andrea was able to work again the following week. She kept herself occupied with jobs that didn't require much physical effort. This helped prevent any further relapses, but the impending second cycle of treatment was having a psychological effect. It loomed on the approaching horizon like a monster lumbering towards her, waiting to swallow her into a pit of stinking blackness.

More blood samples were required on the Wednesday so that the results would be ready for Thursday morning's chemotherapy clinic. Taking blood was something I was trained to do, and we managed to get the samples sent off to the lab without Andrea having to leave work. Thankfully her veins were still in a good condition.

I hadn't noticed, but she told me her hair had started to fall out. There were a few strands balancing precariously where they had fallen onto her shoulders, and when she had woken up that morning there were several clumps cast adrift on her pillow. More than usual had clung to the bristles of her hairbrush when she had brushed it before going to work. This was mentally tough for her, an attack on her femininity, and a threat that was difficult to respond to. The chemotherapy could beat her up as much as it liked, but stealing her hair was beyond cruel.

For a man it would be no problem. For a woman it was different, a bald head wasn't 'normal', and usually meant that she was ill, maybe a cancer sufferer. Hair loss meant there was a chance her illness could cease to be a private matter. How would people respond? Would there be sympathy, pity, misunderstanding, ridicule, avoidance? We hoped the cooling caps had done their job after all, and this was merely a minor blip. We tried to sleep well that night, but the following day's session of chemotherapy was playing on both our minds.

This time we'd made better arrangements for childcare. It wasn't fair for the children to be around in the evening of Andrea's treatment – I couldn't devote enough time to their well-being and look after her, and it wouldn't be pleasant for them to see their mum looking so poorly.

Instead we'd arranged for Kate to collect Hannah from school on Thursday afternoon. Ann would fetch William and keep him with her until Sunday. That gave us three days to get over the worst of the trauma before being needed again as parents.

***

Thursday 15th February 2007

We arrived in plenty of time and Andrea gave her name to 'Charon' before we took our seats in the waiting area. There were faces we recognised, and a few people greeted us as we sat amongst them. Andrea was even included in some of the small talk and general chemo chat with the other women. We weren't the new guys anymore; we had been welcomed amongst the stoics.

We didn't wait long before Andrea was called forward, this time by a nurse we'd not met before. She explained that there was a problem. The blood results had come back as abnormal. The reading for the white cells was too low. This meant giving chemotherapy wasn't possible. Our hearts sank. It seemed as though the treatment would have to be delayed after it had barely started.

However, the nurse explained, the reading on the printout was zero. There were no white cells at all. This result could only have come about due to a machine error, so we were to wait while the sample was re-analysed.

Thankfully, the sample was returned with a value of 6.4, a little higher than two weeks previously when Andrea was feeling terrible. The treatment could continue. The nurse called us through again and we were directed into Dr Purohit's consulting room. He needed to assess Andrea to ensure her fitness for the chemo. The gravelly-honeyed voice deemed her well enough to continue, and then asked how she had faired after the first treatment. He was a little surprised to hear how ill Andrea had been, and decided to increase her anti-sickness drugs.

We returned to the waiting room, but not for long. Lydia appeared and politely asked Andrea if she'd like to follow her (she replied that she wouldn't, but she did it anyway), 'Charon' smiled as we walked past, and we were crossing the Styx for the second time.

Having done this before made it a double edged sword – Andrea knew what to expect and what would happen in Hades, but she also knew what it would do to her, how it would hammer her, make her face her 'sick' demons, and diminish her immunity. I was hugely admiring of her courage and nerve to walk calmly to that seat and sit down for another chemical battering.

Donna Ashley was there once more to support Andrea. She had a useful tip to reduce the sickness – ginger. Ginger tea, ginger biscuits, ginger consumed in any form *should* help. I made a note to get some at the earliest opportunity.

As Lydia slapped, stroked and poked around looking for a suitable vein in Andrea's arm the healthcare assistant arrived with a cooling cap. She asked if there had been any hair loss, and looked hard at Andrea's scalp before saying that she didn't think it had worked. They decided to give it another go. The comedy ice-cream-head-wrestling bout was re-enacted.

Lydia inserted the cannula, and the second cycle began. This went much the same as the first time - a slow, steady infusion of firstly clear, and then pink poison, and then the woozy-alien-dizziness-pins-and-needles backwards plummet into the cyclophosphamide netherworld.

Once again we returned home with Andrea weak and unsteady, and she lay beneath a blanket on the sofa. The queeziness was intense as before, although this time, despite looking awful and writhing in nausea, she managed to avoid actually vomiting.

The rate of hair fall-out was increasing, and strands of the blond bob could be seen wherever she had rested her head. Keeping up with the anti-sickness drugs was again an impossible ordeal. She hadn't improved by the next morning but was trying to eat small amounts of bland food, combined with the ginger. I'd bought some ginger root and made ginger tea with it. This proved unpalatable. However, she was managing to nibble at the ginger biscuits. But no matter how many she forced down the worms still writhed and twisted and spent all day steadily squirming and sliding between her stomach and throat.

The ginger was proving to be powerless, completely lacking in anti-sickness spice.

Saturday was no better, and it was becoming clear that the cooling caps had not worked. When she first raised her head to claw her way slowly out of bed in the morning there appeared to be as much hair on the pillow as on her head. The mirror was starting to lie. The fit, proud, beautiful woman who stood in front of the looking glass bore little resemblance to the pale, balding, ill-looking woman who struggled to stand and stare back. There was hair on her pyjamas and hair on the floor.

This was worse than the sickness, worse than the pain; they were mostly physical sufferings. The pernicious and spiteful hair loss was physically irrelevant, but psychologically destructive. It tore at the fabric of what made Andrea a woman, stole the control over the way she could make herself feel. With a belly full of courage she made a decision, and phoned Marie to come round as soon as she could.

***

Andrea sat on a chair in the kitchen with a towel around her shoulders. Marie stood behind her with her electric clippers in her hand, and asked her for the umpteenth time if she was sure. Andrea said she was, but looked like she wasn't. From the chair she asked if I would rather go somewhere else, somewhere I couldn't watch. But I didn't want to be anywhere else. She was worried that I might not love her as much when Marie had finished, that I might somehow find her to be a different woman.

Marie asked again. Andrea told her to get on with it. Marie flicked the switch and a buzzing resonated around the room. Chunks and strands of hair fell slowly to the floor as Marie pulled the clippers with a slow sweep over Andrea's head from her forehead to the nape of her neck. A broad white furrow of bare scalp appeared like an inverted Mohican. Marie swept again and the furrow widened. Tears of love and pride welled behind my eyes and threatened to blow them across the room. Marie worked on, but looked like she was struggling with her emotions too. As for loving Andrea less, I couldn't possibly have loved her more.

Once again she showed her inner strength as she sat expressionless, occasionally blowing at hairs that annoyingly touched her face on their way to the floor. Mentally she was back with the waiting-room stoics, kicking this disease and its associated ills right where it hurts. She was taking back control. She was in charge. She was going to win this battle.

This felt like seminal moment in her fight against the cancer.

***

Life is an Ultra-marathon

A selection of headscarves had been acquired to adorn the newly shaven head. But such was Andrea's new self-assurance that she rarely wore them. I honestly thought she looked better without one. Her beauty shone through whatever this evil could throw at her, and in my opinion her bare head gave her an attractive confidence. Hannah was unfazed when she returned home and saw her mother with no hair. Four-year-olds seem so adaptable. William was too young to express an opinion, but ran to his mum for cuddles just as often as he always did.

Andrea had grasped the bull by the horns, but there were no such decisive moments in my training. Since the second chemo session I hadn't run, but had undertaken sessions of upper body exercises in the house whenever I had the opportunity. I also wore ankle and wrist weights pretty much constantly.

Looking ahead, I planned to use the daily commute to work to get in some mileage. It occurred to me that if I ran to work, then squeezed in a run at lunchtime, and then ran home from work I'd total nearly a half-marathon distance in one day for little time cost. I tried this when I returned to work on Monday.

It required only a little forward planning and a slight adjustment to the morning routine. I'd made sure I had some shower gel and some clothes to change into stored in my work locker. I set the alarm clock ten minutes earlier, and as soon as it rang I quietly completed the daily stretching routine on the bedroom floor before creeping downstairs and having a light breakfast alone. I wanted to make sure I'd eaten something at least an hour before running, and didn't want to wake everybody else.

The small bowl of cereals I ate was digested while I dressed the children, fed them, brushed their teeth and tried to get Andrea's drugs and a cup of tea into her.

Then at eight o'clock I laced up the trainers and set off into the cold.

Carrying my backpack containing my lunch, I anticipated the four-mile trip across town to take half an hour. Twenty-nine minutes later I strolled into work, strip-washed, and hung my running clothes near the radiator.

The pre-work exercise gave me a lift all morning. I felt lively and full of energy, and it was no problem to rush to the changing room and throw the running kit back on for the second instalment at lunchtime. The speed session was made up of four laps around the perimeter road, and then it was a quick dash back in for another strip-wash and back to work.

I had an energised glow that remained until mid-afternoon, but then my batteries started to feel flat. Five o'clock came around with fatigue hot on its heels. I was not looking forward to more running, but there was no alternative. This made it even better as training, both physically and psychologically - I had to run when I was tired, when I had already run twice that day, and when I had no choice but to pull on the trainers again or I wouldn't get myself back home.

That last run involved training when my muscle glycogen stores were very low; the tank was empty. That wouldn't be a good position in which to start a race, but for ultra training purposes it was excellent. For the Lyke Wake, my body needed to adjust to utilise fat as the main fuel source. Glycogen simply wouldn't last long enough.

The plentiful supply of fat means it is a vital energy source to fire the engine reliably through an ultra-endurance event. The more I trained with low glycogen stores, the more my body was forced to drive on fat, and the better it would become at it. Additionally, when I refuelled after the run, my body would overcompensate and overfill its glycogen store: I could train my fuel tank to become bigger.

There is also the psychological side to low glycogen training: it makes you go slowly, and it is unpleasant if you push hard. Practising slow pacing is a requirement for ultra-running, and being able to continue when it hurts to do so is a pre-requisite.

A concrete heaviness had invaded my leg muscles as I set off home. The first slight uphill had me breathing much heavier than normal, and was holding me back like I was dragging a tyre. This called for a change to ultra tactics – slowing the pace and simply ensuring one foot kept throwing itself in front of the other until I reached home.

The day's training worked well on several levels; it was a long run but also an interval session in an unusual way, a psychological challenge, and also an exercise in loading some of mental software necessary for the planned main event. The same '4+4+4 triple-run' was scheduled in the diary as regular Monday training.

Meanwhile Andrea was working out how best to get through her own ultra-marathon of cancer treatment. Neither of us had any hope of trying to blast through our ordeals in a short, fast sprint. We had to weigh things up, plan a strategy, and keep focused on playing the long game.

Andrea's strategy involved battling the nausea in the short term, trying to get back to work and keep things as normal as possible in the later stages of each chemo cycle, and then to tick each therapy session off one at a time until all six were over. The short-term battle was proving tough, and she showed no improvement in the way she felt until Wednesday – six days after the treatment. But at least the hair issue was back under her control.

In between chipping away at maintaining Andrea's anti-sickness drugs balance, I was chipping away at the training. I managed to squeeze in a couple of short, fast runs with the weighted backpack, and spent some evenings doing upper body exercises and partial squats. The training was becoming a little more regular, despite the traumatic situation that encompassed us.

Even though I wasn't running as often as I would have liked, I was steadily slipping into the habit of making every waking hour some kind of physical challenge, as Mad Dog had taught me in preparation for the coast to coast. I had learnt that you don't always have to run to train for a run.

Eating had crept back on the agenda for Andrea, and we received an invitation to my parent's house for Sunday lunch. This provided another long run opportunity; I made the journey to Sheffield on foot, carrying my weighted backpack, whilst Andrea drove the family in the car.

Life had become a constant act of time management. I had no spare time. I was either in fast-forward or I was sleeping. I had all my usual household chores to do, plus a few extra when Andrea was ill. I also had to go to work (my boss and work colleagues were extremely understanding and helpful, allowing me to arrive a few minutes late and finish a little early when it was necessary), and do my bit for Andrea and the children when I got home. I was still typing away at my coast-to-coast write-up, which was rapidly expanding, and for which I began to harbour bigger ideas. And to top it all, there was an ultra-marathon to train for; and that training was a balancing act between regular running and injury prevention.

I was living enough for two lives. The more I thought about it, life *was* an ultra-marathon. It began to feel that running the Lyke Wake would be taking a rest.

Andrea had some plans of her own for me. This was the year of my 40th birthday, and she wanted to get me a present worthy of an aging fool who doesn't know when to stop running. She asked if I would like a trip to New York to run the marathon. I thought about it for the time it takes a pricked bubble to burst. Hell, yes!

Although my birthday wasn't until June, and the marathon eight months away in November, I was extremely grateful and thrilled. Andrea was also excited. The trip would be long after her treatment had finished, and she would be regaining her strength by then. A few days in New York would be just the tonic to help forget all the woes that were currently befalling her.

The first New York City marathon was run in 1970. This was a small and humble affair, in which 127 runners started the four-and-a-bit laps of Central Park. Only 55 finished. Six years later, the New York Road Runners switched the route to include all five of New York's boroughs, and over 2,000 people entered. The course unites numerous diverse neighbourhoods, crosses five bridges, and finishes at Tavern on the

Green in the south west corner of Central Park

I was a little unsure how I would fare. Hammering the streets of The Big Apple seemed a world away from my natural habitat of open hill and muddy moorland. The surface would be a high impact one, and I do much of my running on soft, uneven stuff. Then there were the pace and gradient to consider – constantly fast and flat. I prefer steep ups and equally steep downs, where the speed regularly alters, and changes occur in the way different muscle groups are used. I was concerned that 26 miles of non-stop fast road running would crack my suspension or cause me to blow a gasket.

Despite being a seasoned runner, I was still a Big-City-Marathon virgin. Many runners, once they get into the sport, quickly set their sights on the challenge of the London Marathon, or the same distance at an event locally; the marathon being a popular benchmark of distance running. I got into running and headed for the hills. But 26.2 miles had been no stranger to me. I had just never done it on tarmac, surrounded by thousands of other runners. I was curious to see how I'd fare running in those conditions.

I completed and sent off an application through a running tours company, *209 Events Ltd*, to run at New York. A few days later I received a telephone call. I could travel with 209 Events, but they had no more guaranteed places for the race. My heart sank. However, the charming lady on the other end of the line informed me that they still had a charity place available, providing I was prepared to run for, and make a small donation to, Cancer Research.

I couldn't think of anything more appropriate. I replied that due to personal circumstances I would endeavour to make the donation significantly more than 'small'. I was invited to join the Cancer Research team.

Vin announced some bad news in late February; he would be unable to join us for the Lyke Wake attempt. He had too many busy weekends at work with the Police force to commit to the challenge. This was a major blow, and I would be without a running partner to blaze a trail with me across the North York moors.

Then another 'friend' made an unwelcome visit: my knee pixie had returned to smite my left leg. Every time I ran downhill I had the sensation of a nail being hammered under the outside edge of my kneecap. I couldn't afford another month off from training. The knee problem needed sorting urgently, once and for all. I contacted my physiotherapist friend, Mick Heys, who invited me to his department the following Friday afternoon.

Mick twisted and pulled my leg, and got me performing several stretching manoeuvres whilst constantly observing my posture. He diagnosed a tight ilio-tibial band. The ilio-tibial band is thickened tissue that stretches down the outside of the thigh from the pelvis to just below the knee. The band is vital in stabilising the knee during running, but if it is too tight it twangs, like a guitar string over the outside edge of the knee, causing the pain I was experiencing.

The good news was that some simple stretches would loosen the band at the pelvis, and cure the knee pain. Mick demonstrated the stretches, and then watched as I attempted them. I could feel an easing sensation as soon as I started.

Mick proved to be a genius once again. He had previously strengthened my partially torn Achilles tendon and got it through the coast-to-coast. And after a week of ITB stretches, the knee pixie fled, never to return.

I was uninjured and pain free, but still unconvinced that I was training appropriately within the time constraints. I whizzed another email to Mad Dog, asking his opinion. If anyone knew what to do, he did. His reply was prompt. His wise words were that I already knew how best to train for the Lyke Wake, because he had taught me, and that I didn't really need him. I wasn't so sure, but I put my faith in his hands, once again.

His words were reassuring for two reasons. The first was that he had confidence in my ability. The second was that he didn't simply take my money in exchange for a program I didn't need. He demonstrated integrity. But that isn't surprising. The rare people like Mad Dog don't do what they do for the money. He doesn't 'make a fast buck'; he knows running is a beautiful freedom, and gently guides people towards it.

I worked on making my training more like a Mad Dog program, and introduced hill sessions into the lunchtime runs. My workplace is situated at the top of a steep road, 200 vertical feet high. This was perfect. Instead of pounding the usual perimeter laps I sprinted down the hill, turned round and jogged steadily back up, before turning round again and repeating the endeavour three more times.

Hill training is an important aspect to running well. It helps build strength and stamina. Practicing on steep gradients would be specific to what I would expect to encounter on the Lyke Wake. But unlike many hill training programs, I'd be following Mad Dog's way: uphill slow and easy, down fast and smooth.

Surprisingly, the downhill sections are more crucial than the uphill. Running hard uphill uses a lot of extra energy for very little return in speed. In the ultra-running energy equation it is too expensive. However, running fast downhill provides a lot of extra speed for little extra energy expenditure. But that doesn't mean it is easy.

When we run down a slope our thigh muscles undergo eccentric contraction. This means that as they contract they get longer rather than shorter. This is very traumatic to the muscles, and tires them quickly. A lot of downhill running can grind an unprepared athlete to a wobbly, weak-legged halt long before the end of an event. Training by speeding down a slope also activates nerve and muscle bundles in such a way that they can improve a runner's general running speed.

My hill training involved practicing going uphill slowly, conserving energy and not overtiring my legs. Then I'd fly downhill, making up for any lost time, training the eccentric contractions and neuro-muscular bundles. This, combined with thousands of partial squats that I was doing at home, was hopefully making my quad muscles bomb-proof.

Running fast down a pavement is very different to speeding down a steep hillside where the surface could be downright dangerous. So I also did the hill training off-road whenever possible, practicing smooth and speedy technique with confidence over the most uneven terrain. I found I excelled at this, and got quite a rush from it.

A consistent pattern was emerging. I was now alternating between lunchtime flat speed sessions and hill sessions without taking time out from family duties, and was combining these with the Monday triple runs to make a more rounded program. Upper body training helped provide total body fitness. Opportunistic long runs at weekends when Andrea felt well enough to child-mind added some confidence that I could run far. But I still wondered, "Exactly how far could I run"?

***

Thursday March 8th 2007

The day of the third bout of chemotherapy came around all too quickly. A routine twice practised but not getting any easier was followed through with courage and determination like the necessary evil that it was. After today the chemo would be half way through, but not the suffering.

We had now become waiting room stoics ourselves, and the procedures were familiar. The first thing was to hear the test results from the blood that I had extracted from Andrea's gradually thinning vein the previous day. The cell counts were lower than we would have liked, but at 5.3 were high enough to continue. Next was the brief consultation with Dr Purohit who was still concerned about the high level of nausea Andrea was experiencing.

Then it was the deep breath, the attempts to calm the fraying nerves, and the sideways glance at the smiling 'Charon' who slowly and deliberately watched our every move as we crossed the Styx for the third time. This time things were slightly different in the chemo suite. No hair, no need to battle with the head-freezing, comical blue helmet. We had also thanked Donna and told her there was no need to give up more time to sit with us - we'd be fine.

Another difference was a change in the prescription for the anti-sickness drugs. Additions to the regime were Motilium suppositories. As these were to be inserted in 'the other end' they couldn't be vomited out and should, in theory, be more effective. They seemed worth a try, at least.

The chemotherapy procedure itself changed little: we sat in different chairs but otherwise we were on repeat. Lydia prodded, poked, and pushed the cannula in Andrea's arm; in went the anti-sickness drug, then the 'F' word, then the glass of rosé, and finally the Cyclophosphamide chaser, which spun her round and pulled her backwards into its unique theme-park-from-hell-like assortment of unpleasant rides and experiences.

Then we had the same pained trundle back home, and the same weekend of playing cat-and-mouse with queasiness and hide-and-seek with the newly extended anti-emetic drug regime. At least this time hair loss wasn't an issue.

The Motilium proved difficult and unpleasant. This was not only due to the disagreeable practice of actually getting the little torpedos in, but also Andrea found they caused diarrhoea and painful stomach cramping. So, adding to the endless cascade of pharmacology, she was prescribed Loperamide to fight diarrhoea, which she could take as often as needed, and buscopan tablets to relieve the muscle cramps, which were taken three times a day.

So, now there were two drugs to counteract the diarrhoea and the stomach cramps that were caused by several drugs to prevent the nausea that was caused by the three drugs used to kill the disease that may or may not actually still be present. It was becoming an insane, neverending spiral of cause and effect, like a rabid dog frantically chasing its tail faster and faster into madness. Just like the 'old lady who swallowed a fly' Andrea was now on to swallowing the cat. I just hoped we never got to the horse.

Andrea wasn't physically sick after the third chemotherapy. However, she did still feel nauseous, and all Friday and Saturday she felt generally far more ill and more fatigued than on the previous occasions. Then things changed.

The first three dreadful days were followed by a spectacular bounce-back. She awoke on the Sunday morning feeling hungry. Ravenously hungry! I drove her to a local diner, and she ordered a steak dinner. This was wolfed down as if it never touched the sides, and was followed by a voluminous dessert. It was a relief to see. I wasn't sure if the eating was due to her body gaining in strength and fighting back, or simply a response to starvation resulting from the dramatic decrease in food uptake over the preceding weeks.

Whatever the reason, it was having a marvellous effect. The rate of recovery was wonderful. Not only did she pick up comfortably enough to go back to work eleven days after the treatment, but two days later I found her on the living room floor doing sit-ups. I couldn't believe it. She seemed inspired, motivated to battle back to full strength; she had a body full of fight.

After just another two days she pulled on her running shoes, and we set out for a family jog, albeit a slow and short one. I pushed William in his pushchair, Hannah rode her bike, and we all followed Andrea for a wonderful two miles around the edge of the local woods. I was delighted, and hugely admiring of her strength and resolve, but at the same time cautious that she might have been pushing too hard.

I needn't have worried. Three days later, on the eve of the fourth cycle of chemotherapy, she ran again.

***

Spring

The hospital workforce review had removed Andrea's job, but four new posts were being created for Assistant Practitioners in radiography within the imaging department. The job would involve performing a range of X-rays on patients, and was at a pay band higher than the one she was currently on. A year of in-post training and studying at University would be required, which didn't fill Andrea with glee, but she applied, and was successful. Every change and every threat presents an opportunity.

I was still taking every opportunity to run in my lunch breaks. I skipped through the doors into a bright and blustery March midday, gradually picked up the pace, rounded three corners, and ran, almost literally, into another runner who was bounding in the opposite direction. He was Alan Ward, a physiotherapist and friend of mine. In the past he had been helpful with my running injuries, and it was he who had got me in touch with his colleague, Mick.

Alan was also out for a lunchtime training session, and changed his planned route to join me. We chatted as we ran. Or rather, he chatted whilst I gasped, desperately trying to keep up with the blistering pace he was setting. Alan was a strong runner; he performed well in the many fell races he entered, and was the captain of Dark Peak fell-running club. He stood about as tall as myself, at six feet, but was more lithe and chiselled, and must have weighed a good fifteen pounds less.

After a mile following my route into the streets around the hospital, Alan offered to show me some nearby trails, knowing we both preferred to blast through hills and woodland. I accepted, and followed him as he powered down a grassy lane before leading into a copse of trees that I never knew existed.

That opportunistic meeting with Alan proved serendipitous. I started to run with him regularly. He showed me many off-road trails within a short distance of the hospital, some steep, some winding, in woodland,

and through fields; and with the knowledge of these paths I found I rarely needed to pound the tarmac on my lunchtime runs anymore.

But better still, running with Alan was tough, and extremely good training. He was faster than me: stronger up the hills, and had a sharper turn of speed in a sprint. He always ran in studded fell shoes, which gripped and clawed at the ground. I would try to follow his fast pace up steep trails, but he'd shoot off skywards, his shoes tearing at the earth and spraying it back at me like I was vainly attempting to chase a moto-cross bike with the rider opening the throttle.

I returned from every session panting hard, my heart thumping through my chest, and my leg muscles screaming to sit down. There was only one area I could keep up with him: downhill.

Alan always had an idea of how to turn every run into a valuable training session. One day it would be hill sprints; every time the road or trail went uphill we ran hard, taking it easy on the flats and downs (Mad Dog wouldn't approve). The next time he'd flip it: we'd go easy uphill: then sprint down like kamikazes. Another time it would be minute sprints: we'd use his stopwatch and sprint for 60 seconds; and then jog easy for 60 seconds to recover (actually, he'd jog easy for 60 seconds to recover, whilst I tried to slow down but still catch him up ready for the next sprint). Other times we'd start the run at a moderate pace, but gradually and continuously increase the effort until we were blazing for home, giving the final hundred metres 100% effort.

Occasionally we'd take it easy, and enjoy the view and the chat. This was usually if Alan had raced within the previous day or two. On one such pleasant run we were snaking our way through woodland on a new trail. I was following close on Alan's heels, not paying too much attention. He ducked under a thick tree branch, and I didn't. There were two loud thuds, the second of which was me hitting the ground. The world spun for a few moments. Blood from the wound on my forehead mingled with sweat, and ran down my face and into my left eye. I was able to continue and run back to work, but as I walked down the corridors to the changing room I looked like an extra who hadn't made it to the end of a Quentin Tarantino film. As I returned through the hospital several people, patients and staff alike, tried to direct me to the emergency department, thinking I was an injured patient.

***

Wednesday March 28th 2007

The day of the fourth bout of chemotherapy arrived, and Andrea was feeling stronger and ready for the fight. In the other corner of the ring stood the new challenger: a different drug, at a different hospital, on a different day. Taxotere was licensed to be administered at Weston Park Hospital in Sheffield, and this would be given to Andrea on Wednesdays.

Taxotere was first made from the needles of the yew tree. Like the FEC agents, it works by stopping cancer cells from dividing. But, also like FEC, it does this to healthy cells too. It is a liquid that is infused slowly through a drip over the course of an hour or so. One serious potential problem with Taxotere is that it can cause an allergic reaction, potentially leading to anaphylactic shock. This is prevented by taking a high dose of dexamethasone steroid tablets for two days, starting the day before treatment.

Weston Park Hospital is located in a very busy part of Sheffield, just to the west of the city centre. It isn't difficult to get to from where we live on the western edge of Chesterfield. In fact we can get there using a beautifully scenic route that skirts the edge of the Peak District, and this takes no longer than the 45 minutes required for the hectic, mind-numbing, direct urban drive from town to city.

What *is* difficult is parking the car once you get there. The hospital is a major regional cancer centre, and its car park is woefully small considering the large number of patients that travel long distances for regular treatment there. But this first time we were lucky; someone pulled out of one of the small number of on-street parking spaces just up the road, and I nipped into the gap. We weren't sure how long the treatment would take, so I loaded the parking meter with as much money as I could, and made a note of the time when I'd have to return.

The hospital was vastly different from the Cavendish Suite at Chesterfield. It was much larger, and extremely busy. The front doors, set back and raised above the road, opened into an entrance hall that appeared to be the focus of frantic activity, but amongst it were areas of seating, oases of stillness, that were full of patients and relatives, waiting their turn to be called to join the madness. A news-stand and a small tea shop squeezed the proceedings into an even tighter space.

We found our way to the stairwell and up the stairs to the appropriate clinic: and we waited. Quite some time passed before we were invited into a small consulting room whose window faced out onto the busy road a few floors below. This was unlike Mr Holt's consulting room; it certainly wasn't new, the decor was stuck in a previous decade, and the open window that let in a cocktail of cool draft and street noise looked like it wouldn't shut without a fight.

Sitting with his back to the stubborn, cold-looking aluminium window frame was another member of Dr Purohit's team, Dr Thanvi. He read Andrea's case notes and asked questions. We listened, tried to translate his accent, and answered as best we could. He explained the plan: there would be three cycles of Taxotere, three weeks apart. The first would be today. Had Andrea remembered to take the extra dexamethasone?

Had Andrea remembered to do what? Extra dexamethasone, no. Should she have?

Dr Thanvi looked at us in a manner that said what his lack of English popular culture quotations couldn't: "Houston, we have a problem".

"Weren't you given some extra steroids to take yesterday?" he queried.

"No....I don't know.......I don't think so..." was our most decisive reply.

What we did have at home was a polythene bag full of bottles of anti-emetics, steroids, suppositories, antacids and pain killers, and a confusing list as long as the flight of stairs we had just walked up detailing when and how to take them. We also had two small children who grab things and stuff them in their mouths, so the bag was kept mostly hidden. Did we have extra dexamethasone and instructions to take it yesterday? We really couldn't be certain, but we didn't think so. Maybe.

The Taxotere couldn't be given today. Without the protection of the steroids, the risk of anaphylactic shock, and potentially sudden death, was too high. Dr Thanvi thought for a minute, and then left the room. Andrea and I looked at each other. We vaguely remembered Lydia saying something about dexamethasone during the last chemo, but 'vaguely' was all we had to go on. Wednesday was Taxotere day; we were facing a week's delay for the treatment.

Dr Thanvi returned, sat down, and said there was a possible solution. If they could get some dexamethasone for Andrea to take now, they would be able to adjust things so that she could return for the Taxotere tomorrow. It would be difficult for them to arrange, but not impossible. We were very grateful, apologised in case the oversight was our fault, and waited in the clinic seating area for the tablets to be delivered. The wait was a lengthy one, but we were relieved that the treatment could still go ahead with only a day's delay.

As we returned up the street to the car, Dr Purohit came walking down the pavement towards the hospital. He recognised us.

"Hello, my dear. Finished already? How's it gone?" the honeyed-gravel enquired.

"It's not gone," replied Andrea, and we recounted the events to him.

He looked angry, saying that we should have received written instruction from the hospital telling Andrea to take the dexamethasone. We certainly hadn't received any such letter. He stormed off towards the hospital, growling with far more gravel and far less honey.

We returned the next day, and were surprisingly fortunate in finding a street parking space again. We hoped the alternative arrangements that Dr Thanvi had initiated had been successful. Andrea rattled with a belly full of steroid tablets that had prevented her from sleeping. The high dose of steroids had given her nocturnal restless legs, and all night she twitched, wriggled and shuffled as if she was trying to run the 10K race we never got to.

The same staircase led us back to the same clinic, and we were relieved to find the staff expecting us. Andrea was led into a treatment room that was twice the size of the one in Chesterfield, but contained nearly four times as many chairs. Space was at a premium. The decor was less harsh than Dr Thanvi's consulting room, but the view through the window was less pleasant; a concrete building loomed close, blocking out much of the sky. The nurse directed Andrea to a vacant seat, explained what would happen, checked her details and swiftly inserted the cannula.

A line was connected from the cannula and onto the bottom of a bag that hung limply above Andrea's head from a stainless steel stand. A machine similar to the one used for William's treatment measured the rate of flow of the drug. Andrea would have to sit for an hour whilst the bag steadily drained the clear Taxotere into her vein.

I was curious whether this drug would have an early effect on Andrea, and watched her like she was a movie unfolding in front of me. She sat still, occasionally flipping the pages of a glossy magazine. Time passed slowly.

Drip...drip...drip. Flip... flip. Tick... tick went the clock on the wall above the door.

I felt like I was sitting next to a time bomb that could explode into who knows what at any moment.

Drip...drip...drip...Flip, flip. Tick..drip..tick..drip.. The suspense was killing me.

The bag emptied, and we waited for it to be disconnected. It was a long wait. The staff at Weston Park found it difficult to keep up with the busy workload. It was probably a further half an hour before the nurse returned to check Andrea and the bag. Once happy that all was fine, she removed the spent equipment, and said we were free to leave. And that was it.

The first dose of Taxotere, and fourth bout of chemotherapy was done. There had been no explosion, no alien queasiness, and no ill effects. We walked steadily back to the car, wondering whether the hardest part of the battle had passed. But Taxotere's effects were to prove to be pernicious.

Over the course of the next day I watched Andrea gradually fade into exhaustion like the batteries in an over-used child's toy. Another uncomfortable, sleepless night hadn't helped. There was no sickness, no nausea, just tiredness; a deep, dark, unrelenting, life-sapping tiredness.

The tiredness continued and increased in intensity, and was joined by a reddening of her skin. This was all over her body, and it felt hot, like bad sunburn. This was a reaction we didn't expect; a poison toxic glow.

The toxic glow lasted three days, but the exhaustion persisted and was joined by a raging sore throat and a rasping cough. An infection was taking hold of a body whose immunity had been pounded for ten straight weeks. June bundled Andrea into her car and drove her back to Weston Park. The doctors had a good prod and poke, looked in her throat, and analysed Andrea's blood yet again. The white cell levels were near the bottom end of normal range. The iron level was also low.

Andrea was sent home with a course of antibiotics, some iron tablets, and instructions to rest, and drink plenty of fluids. The antibiotic, called erythromycin, confused the anti-sickness drug regime still further, especially as the antacids were to be avoided whilst taking the antibiotics.

She was also advised to avoid contact with anyone who had an infection. We had two children at home, who were both like a walking source of plague. One went to school, the other to nursery, and both brought home whatever germs were going around the other children. Avoiding infections was going to be almost impossible.

***

By April the Lyke Wake plans were in full swing. Mal and I had booked the accommodation for everyone, having gambled on Andrea's treatment running to time and finishing on July 20th. After a long and annoying wrestling match with his healing processes, Mal's collarbone was once again up to the stresses of off-road cycling. It had taken thirteen weeks for the shards of bone to grow sticky and fuse together, and another couple of months before he felt it strong and safe enough to risk throwing his leg over a bike. But the bone hadn't glued itself smoothly, and a sharp point could be felt just under the skin.

Spring had stolen some of summer's weather, and April showed off by blazing an unseasonably hot sun down on northern England for several weeks. Temperatures soared, and the ground baked hard and cracked. We were making preparations for the Lyke Wake to be a blisteringly hot ordeal; most of our discussions were about how best to avoid sunburn and heatstroke whilst battling across the exposed North York Moors. We couldn't have imagined how wrong we would be

But in the meantime the program of life played only repeats. The weather repeated very hot and sunny. Andrea, this time taken by June, repeated the trip to Weston Park. They repeated the hour's drip, drip, flip, flip, and then the half hour's wait to be unshackled from the empty bag. Back home the fade into the blackness of exhaustion was repeated, and was followed quickly by another hot, red toxic glow.

This time, the infection that dragged Andrea back to the hospital for a check-over was caused by blood results that were lower still. The doctor's expressions displayed more unease than they had previously. They didn't like the way the chemotherapy was now knocking Andrea down with every hit. But there was nothing to do but repeat the antibiotic prescription and repeat the advice to rest.

But at least we were now five treatments down, only one to go.

***

The final chemotherapy treatment was administered on Wednesday 9th May 2007, and the relief after the bag and the needle had been removed was almost tangible. I gave Andrea a long hug, proud of her bravery and single-minded determination to get through the horrors. It had been awful, but she hadn't wavered. It was now a case of ploughing stubbornly through the tiredness and the toxic glow, regaining strength, and getting into the starting blocks for the six-week run of radiotherapy.

We should have been able to predict what would happen. The recurring pattern had been there for all to see. The blood results were progressively lower before each cycle of chemotherapy, and lower still every time Andrea developed the seemingly inevitable post-treatment infection.

But foolishly, we *didn't* predict the infection, and when it took hold there was nobody to drive her to Weston Park to be examined. June and Geoff were away, and I was at work. Andrea drove herself, which couldn't have been easy in her fatigued state. When she arrived there weren't any parking spaces, and she had to trawl the back streets slowly for half an hour before she found somewhere to leave the car. That was half a mile away from the hospital, and she had no option but to walk. When she finally battled her way into the clinic she was exhausted.

The doctors were more concerned than at any previous time. Andrea was spiking a high temperature of 39 degrees, and the concern increased when the blood results were returned. The white cell levels were below the normal range, reading only 2.4. The worry was that her biological defences were now so depleted that the infection could thrive and develop almost unchecked.

A discussion ensued about whether to admit Andrea onto one of the wards to give her a blood transfusion. She didn't want that. She wanted to be at home, and argued that another course of antibiotics would be sufficient. She was also worried that she would get a parking ticket for leaving the car beyond the time on the meter, but didn't mention that as she didn't think it would cut much ice with the medical staff. Andrea narrowly won the debate, but was warned that if she began to feel any worse, even a tiny bit, then she had to return urgently.

She didn't worsen; she fought, and she improved.

***

Tuesday 29th May 2007

Today was the start of things new for Andrea: a new job and a new treatment plan. This was her first day in training as an assistant practitioner in radiography. There would be no more typing and secretarial work. From now on, work would be centred on taking X-rays. And in the twists and turns of the irony of life, the cancer treatment would from now onwards involve her being bombarded with X-rays. She was nervous, but nervous and normal were beginning to feel one and the same.

The appointment with the oncologist came first thing in the morning, before work. We were directed to another part of Weston Park hospital, where radiotherapy planning took place. Dr Purohit explained the purpose of the radiotherapy, and its potential side-effects. Side effects were something we had become close to: as the saying goes, "Keep your friends close, but your enemies closer". We wanted to know what radiotherapy could possibly inflict that the chemo hadn't managed to. Andrea was cautious of everything, but beginning to fear nothing.

The radiotherapy was to reduce the risk of the cancer recurring. Radiation would be fired at Andrea's breast from a machine called a linear accelerator. This would destroy any cancer cells within the treated area. It would also destroy normal cells, but the body's natural healing response should repair those tissues over time. Each treatment, known as a *fraction*, would be given to the breast daily from Monday to Friday, for five weeks. Giving the treatment in fractions reduces the damage to normal cells. Then there would be an extra sixth week where the treatment would be focused on the scar area, from where the original lump had been removed.

There would be two main side effects to watch out for. The first would be tiredness, which would be worsened by having to make the daily travel to and from Weston Park hospital. Tiredness could even be a problem for several months after the treatment had finished. Secondly, three or four weeks into the radiotherapy, reddening and soreness of the skin could develop; and there may be some discomfort and swelling of the breast. The skin would develop hypersensitivity to sunlight, and for at least the first year after radiotherapy the treated area should be covered up when outside in strong sunshine. But all of that sounded like a walk in the park compared with the recently experienced horrors of chemotherapy. Bring it on.

After Dr Purohit had finished his explanation, we were invited to sit back in the waiting area. Andrea would be invited into another room for treatment planning. The seating stretched down the middle of a long, wide chamber that was almost a corridor leading to the radiotherapy treatment centre. Clinical and examination rooms opened out into the light waiting area. But more brightness shone from the treatment suite at the far end, almost symbolic of the beams of radiation that were being produced there.

It was very busy, but we found two seats next to each other, and sat for the wait that proved to be lengthy. Radiotherapy treats many different types of cancer, and many people of all ages, shapes and sizes came to wage their involuntary war. They wandered in, sat, waited, talked, had consultations, drank coffee, waited some more, had treatment, recognised friends, talked some more, stared out of the window, and many smiled. There they were again: the smiles. Smiles and optimism. There was something about being struck by this disease that stoked the fire of human resilience and determination. Everyone there was a team. Not just the hospital staff, but all the patients and relatives as well. Team Recovery. Team Hope.

Over half an hour of people-watching passed before Andrea was called into a treatment planning room. Two radiotherapists positioned her on a treatment couch that simulated how the linear accelerator would be set up. Light beams were shone at Andrea's breast, showing where the X-rays would be fired. Several times Andrea was moved into different positions, and the beams were altered. Dr Purohit regularly popped in to have a look, before disappearing again. The therapists had to ensure the equipment would be set up to treat all the necessary area, but minimise irradiating surrounding healthy tissue, especially the lungs. It was a lengthy process, during which time I waited and watched more and more members of Team Hope come and go.

When Dr Purohit was happy, several lines were drawn on Andrea's skin using a marker pen. These were to ensure the treatment X-ray beam would be aligned exactly the same way as the planning set-up. Andrea was not to wash these marks off her skin. They would be needed for the next two months.

***

Saturday 9th June 2007

Nearly five weeks separated the final chemotherapy session and the start of the radiotherapy. This gave Andrea an extra two weeks of recovery and strengthening time before beginning the tiresome daily journey to Sheffield to be blasted with radiation. The weekend of my 40th birthday fell at the end of this settling period.

Andrea had surprised me with a night away to celebrate. After watching the children leave with Ann on Saturday morning, we drove into the Peak District and relaxed with a pub-lunch next to the graceful River Derwent as it meandered its way from the High Peak, past Hathersage, and down towards the Chatsworth Estate.

Then we laced up our walking boots and set off for a stroll. Fair weather enchanted the river; regular gaps in the clouds revealed warming summer sunlight that danced a celebratory jig on the gentle currents massaging the roots of the overhanging trees. We weren't going far; Andrea couldn't. Tiredness washed over her easily, and her previous athletic runner's physique had been atrophied and re-shaped by enforced inactivity and too many steroids. But she did what she did, and it was marvellous.

We ambled slowly for two miles along the riverbank, before turning south-westwards up the hillside towards Offerton Hall. The hill was steep, but only 500 yards long. Andrea was forced to walk very slowly, and stopped three times on the small climb. Her fitness levels before the chemotherapy would have enabled her to run up the slope non-stop. So far the cancer treatment had been brutal and exhausting, stripping Andrea of many of the physical attributes that made her what she was. She completed the four mile walk at a steady pace, and together we marvelled at some of the magnificent scenery that pumped joy and happiness into our souls. We vowed to run together there one day. It was still a beautiful world.

***

Monday 11th June 2007

The beauty was less evident two days later as Marie drove Andrea back to Weston Park for the first of 30 hits of radiotherapy. As usual, there were no parking spaces, so Marie dropped Andrea off at the door, and arranged to meet her once she had parked.

In the radiotherapy suite, Andrea was invited into a cubicle and asked to change into a gown. She was given a basket in which to put her clothes and valuables. Then she sat back in the waiting area, keeping the basket with her.

The suite was as busy and bright as it had been previously, as if lit by optimism, the Team's rays of hope, and the machine's rays of cure. This was where people took their cancer to be killed.

Marie arrived and sat with Andrea moments before she was called into the treatment room. Andrea's gown was removed to uncover her from the waist up, and she lay on the treatment couch. The head of the linear accelerator was brought over her chest. A beam of light shone out from the machine, showing the radiotherapist exactly where the beam of X-rays would strike Andrea. Time was spent ensuring that the alignment was perfect, in exactly the correct position that had been determined on the day of the treatment planning.

Then, when the set-up was complete, the radiotherapist left the area, and Andrea had to remain still whilst the therapy beam was switched on. There were no dramatic noises or flashing lights, this was silent assassination.

No more than ten minutes later, the radiotherapist returned and told Andrea that they had finished. She could get dressed and go. Andrea hadn't felt anything; there was no pain, no discomfort. It was really easy.

The procedure was exactly repeated every time, but the driver taking Andrea to and from the hospital changed. On Tuesday and Wednesday it was my mother, June. Then on Thursday it was another friend of Andrea's, Cathy Butler. We had many people helping us, for which we were extremely grateful. Without them we would have struggled terribly. A pattern emerged: Marie driving on Mondays, June on Tuesdays and Wednesdays, Cathy helping out later in the week, and then near the end of the six weeks, another friend, Sue Southern, kindly gave up her time and petrol.

***

Monday 25th June 2007

Following April's theft of some of the summer sun, the month of June couldn't afford to pay its dues. It became powerless to stop a deluge that turned out to be the heaviest single day's rainfall on record. At work the rain sounded like the drummers from a hundred marching bands practising their rhythms on the roof. The River Rother that flows through Chesterfield dramatically flooded, cutting it off with an east-west divide. The hospital is east of the river; we live to the west. The M1 motorway, also to the east, became flooded and was closed. All the traffic travelling on the country's main artery was diverted into Chesterfield.

Gridlock and chaos ensued. The traffic from both carriageways of the M1 met each other at the river at the bottom of the hill below the hospital. At the end of the day shift there was nowhere to go, no way for drivers to get home. Many people spent eight hours or more sitting in their cars going nowhere, while the rain still hammered down.

I was fortunate. I had gone to work on a motorbike, and managed to weave through the gridlock, find a way across and onto the west side. There, the roads were deserted. There was only my motorbike and me, and fountains blowing upwards through every street grate.

Fortunately, Andrea had reached Weston Park and had her treatment before the river burst its banks, but she couldn't get home from work, and my babysitting mother couldn't get home to Sheffield. I phoned Andrea on her mobile and told her to abandon the car, and I set off on the motorbike to rescue her. The rescue was wet and slow, but successful.

Into the night we heard that the roads were beginning to clear. We needed the car back for the following day's radiotherapy. I quickly pulling on my running clothes and set out into the wet night. I jogged, splashed and half-swam across town, picking my route to avoid the deepest water – some of the underpasses would have required scuba diving gear. The car rescue was successful, and fun.

Having a good fitness level and a thirst for adventure has its advantages.

Slowly and steadily, the radiotherapy was grinding Andrea down. It was almost too gradual to notice, but her energy levels and liveliness weakened like a fading summer sunset. Life had carried on as normal for the first two weeks, but then exhaustion set in, and feeling drained and stressed, she had to stop going to work.

The radiation burns began to appear after four weeks. These first manifested as a sore red area on her right breast, but progressively worsened as the treatment continued. The sore areas broke open and began to weep. She was prescribed creams to apply: firstly an aqueous cream, and then one which contained silver. Advice was also given to allow air to get to the burns; she was told to lie on the bed with the sore area uncovered and the window open.

***

Saturday July 14th 2007

The week before the Lyke Wake, with only five more days of treatment remaining, Andrea was happy for me to go and run a 10Km trail race in Sherwood Pines, near Mansfield. She stayed at home with the children, and I rode to the race on the motorbike through a nice, bright day. A few light clouds ambled across a big sky. The weather had been like this for several days, and all signs of the recent flooding had vanished. Everywhere was dry, the ground was firm, and I didn't expect any mud on the trails.

Without a car to get changed in I prepared for the race before leaving home. I was vaselined up, wearing nip-guards, and sporting shorts and vest under my warmer biking clothes.

The venue was beautiful: a sizeable forested area that contained a warren of bike trails and walking paths, in Nottinghamshire, close to Robin Hood country.

I chained the bike to a fence by a tree, stripped down to my running clothes and headed for the start area. There were a couple of hundred runners waiting to get going. After eyeing many of them up, I felt confident of a good run, and positioned myself right at the front.

There was a brief countdown from ten to zero, and we were off, blasting along trails that snaked and undulated through the trees. The surface was mostly dusty, which was kicked up by our pounding shoes, and I was pleased to be breathing the fresh air at the front of the race rather than choking at the back. Several sandy sections had us all slipping, sliding and slowing the pace, which would have caused bottlenecks further back.

The race was a combined 5km and 10km race, made up of two loops that crossed through a single finish area. I was running well. There were only a handful out in front of me after three kilometres, and they were all within sight as we dropped down the first descent.

The gaps had widened slightly as we approached the finish area the first time around. I hoped that some of the runners ahead were in the

5km race, but they all blazed through to start the second lap. I wasn't catching any of them, but I was pleased to think that had I been running the 5km race, I would have won it.

The fast, fluid pace was maintained throughout the second lap, but I couldn't catch anyone ahead. Instead, with 1km to go I could sense someone close behind me. He had been hunting me since the start of the second loop, but without success. There were only six runners ahead of me, and I knew there was a good chance that I was the leader of the veteran's category. I didn't want to get caught. The trail ahead descended slightly before turning and climbing a short but steep rise to the finish.

If I continued to go hard all the way there was a chance I'd fade and get passed by my pursuer. Instead I adopted a strategy that had an element of risk. With two hundred yards to go before the final climb, I eased off the gas very slightly. This wasn't enough to make my plan obvious, but it gave me a little rest; just enough. In doing so I gave my chaser just a snippet of hope, an inkling of belief that he could beat me.

I sensed him increase his effort as he believed me to be there for the taking. Approaching the bottom of the hill I had allowed him to claw to within a few paces, but I could hear he was panting hard, blasting air in and out of his lungs like a steam train pulling with all its might.

We turned the final left had bend, almost together. The steam train had given everything to get on my shoulder, while I had coasted and saved some energy for the late explosion. I kicked hard, giving everything in those first hundred metres of the climb. It hurt like hell. I was blowing like a hurricane, but the steam train had hit the buffers as soon as I hit the gas. He had spent everything to catch me, and had nothing left to race with. He was beaten, physically and psychologically. I ran hard round the last bend, and looked behind with 50 metres to go. There were no chasing trains, no runners, just my dust settling.

Brains and brawn had come together, and man, that felt fantastic. My race time was good; better than I had hoped for at 39 minutes. I had finished the race seventh overall, but sadly I wasn't the first veteran. I had to settle for second in category.

With my body glowing with effort and satisfaction, I ambled back to the car park, pulled off my shirt and stood next to the bike, cooling off. Curiously, I appeared to be the subject of numerous strange looks from other people as they walked by. Children pointed and laughed. Adults stared and raised eyebrows. I couldn't figure it out. Then I looked down and realised: I was still wearing my nip guards. I guess it's not usual for men to stand topless in a car park with their nipples taped up.

***

Robin Hood's Bay

Andrea came out from the hospital, walked calmly across the road, and sat beside me in the car. And that was that.

The treatment was over. No more abuse, no more insult, no more surgery, poisoning, nausea or radiation. But no celebrations, cheering or flag-waving either! Somehow it seemed something of an anticlimax, as if the guns had just fallen silent at the end of wartime hostilities, and the ensuing calm felt eerie and uncomfortable. As if it was once again safe to walk the bombed-out city streets, and begin rebuilding. Andrea had rebuilding to do also. Physical scars, radiation burns and soreness would take time to heal, and hair several months to grow back. Energy levels would take time to return to normal, as would her physique. The battle was over, but had the war been won? How long could the ceasefire last? We wouldn't know for many years, years trying not to worry and look over our shoulders at the smouldering rubble of lives troubled by cancer.

"Fancy a coffee?" Andrea piped up. "There's a Starbucks just up the road. I could go and get us a couple of lattes for the journey".

"Great idea," I replied, and shouted, "and a piece of cake," through the car window as she headed back out of sight.

I sat for a few more minutes, loaded a CD into the stereo and watched the busy world frantically carry out its normal insanity up and down the streets of Sheffield. Within five minutes Andrea returned with two large take-away cups of coffee and an even larger chocolate chip cookie. She fastened her seatbelt and we pulled away. Without so much as a glance over our shoulders at the hospital, we headed for Robin Hood's Bay. The mental and physical anguish was left slowly fading into the distance behind us; our destination was one of our favourite places in the world, the beautiful Yorkshire fishing village where I proposed to her.

The two-and-a-half hour journey was uneventful apart from the memorable sense of relief. We reached Robin Hood's Bay just after lunchtime, parked the car at the top of the very steep hill and had an easy stroll down the few hundred yards to the slipway by the old coastguard's station. The weather was bitterly cold for July with slight rain in the air, and this invoked even more memories of the pained limp down the vicious hill, through heavy drizzle, under leaden skies to the finish of the coast-to-coast. We had always loved this little village but now it was becoming a place of iconic proportion; something significant always seemed to happen here. It was the destination of one of our first holidays, we got engaged here, finished the ultra-marathon here, now we came here immediately after Andrea's cancer treatment, and would leave here for the longest single day's running I had ever done.

I had to eat to fill my body's fuel tank for tomorrow's efforts – the Lyke Wake run. We chose to lunch in the Bay Hotel. Whilst we ate, several text messages were exchanged between the members of the Respect The Stupidity team who, except for Vin, were all making their way to join us. Despite his absence Vin was involved in the text tennis, and he wished all our souls well for their 'long and arduous journey over Whinny Moor'.

After lunch Andrea and I wandered slowly around the village, relaxing properly for the first time in many months, and soaking up the calm, untroubled, timeless atmosphere of our spiritual second home. But despite being mid-summer it was too cold to hang around aimlessly. It was as if the weather was trying to hustle us away, to gently push us somewhere else. We walked back to the car and drove the twelve-mile journey inland and round the bay to Raven Hall Hotel.

One sight of the dramatic, grey, stone-built hotel and its rugged entrance brought memories of the end of the coast-to-coast flooding back. There stood the rotating wooden and glass door that had previously proven so difficult to get through with my large kit bag. In front of them were the three stone steps that angered my knee pixie on every descent, and the stainless steel wheelchair-ramp that I would undoubtedly have used on the previous visit had I had a wheelchair. Even the weather repeated that of the prior stay. I knew to attack the steps rather than risk the wheelchair ramp that ought to bear a sign reading 'slippery when wet'.

This time, however, I was dressed for the cool weather instead of shivering in damp, muddy running gear, and so felt comfortable rather than conspicuous in the traditionally appointed and nicely carpeted lobby area. To our left a well-to-do elderly couple were taking afternoon tea in the lounge. The gentleman was deeply entrenched in his copy of *The Times*. The lady glanced over and smiled. I smiled back as Andrea and I walked towards reception to check-in. Our room was on the first floor, so I was able to re-enact the struggle with the wide carpeted steps that arced up and round in a semicircle from the lobby. Our room was only three doors away from the family room that subjected us to our sleep-deprived night of nauseating, vomit-riddled torture. We opened the door, walked inside, and it felt comfortable.

After dropping the bags on the floor we stepped over to the window and stared at the same view over the sea to Robin Hoods Bay. A few hardy souls had taken to the sands, most exercising their dogs, but one or two children buzzed around rock pools with their fishing nets, their parents trying to hide from the elements and looking like they'd rather be somewhere else. We didn't want to be anywhere else. We had just escaped from 'somewhere else', and it had been a frightening, sickness making, troublesome 'somewhere else'; a world of pain, surgery, drugs and radiation.

Looking westwards from the window the hill adjacent to the hotel rose a couple of hundred feet, and at the top stood a radio mast pointing stubbornly towards the ominous sky. This effectively marked the end of the Lyke Wake route. It would be visible from many miles away and would help guide me to the finish. From the mast all I had to do was jog down a path through a field and onto a narrow lane that joined the small road to the hotel. I sat on the bed studying the map and comparing features with those I could see on the hill. The path I needed could be seen in the grassy field. It felt good to have a bit of homework completed, and I felt confident that I'd have no trouble navigating the last few miles to the hotel. All I had to worry about was the not insignificant task of hauling myself across 40 miles of moorland first. I tried not to think about such a technicality, and instead suggested to Andrea that we went to the bar for a relaxing drink. She agreed.

The wood-panelled bar area was almost empty and we sat at a table in a far corner. My telephone chimed as it received a message from Mal and Andrea saying they were half an hour away. As we waited, the bar gradually filled with hotel guests, the men all dressed in suits and the women in posh frocks. A wedding was taking place in the hotel and, judging from the accents of the majority of the guests, they had travelled from the northeast, probably Newcastle. The barman was very busy. It looked like being a lively evening.

Mal and Andrea arrived, and it was a joy to see them, as it was when Justin and Andy appeared ten minutes later. The more we chatted with our friends away from the world of treatment we had left behind, the more that previous life seemed distant, unreal even. Yet Andrea's soreness and physical scars prevented complete escapism. We discussed tomorrow's weather forecast, which was for a cold, cloudy, rainy day, before heading back to our rooms to wash and dress for dinner.

The hotel food was extremely good. Justin, Mal and myself ate well, and as much as we could, choosing a high carbohydrate intake to overload our glycogen stores, before heading to our rooms for an early night. But it started to look like another restless night would be had at Raven Hall. The wedding guests weren't interested in our quality of sleep. Many of them had been drinking hard for several hours, and at 11 o'clock that night the karaoke started right under our bedroom.

Drunken Geordies went all-out at their unofficial *X-Factor* audition, cheered on by a rowdy crowd of friends, family and no doubt distant relatives. A pillow over my head proved a futile weapon in defending my ears from a shockingly out-of-key 'Delilah'. Like Tom Jones I was left wondering "Why, Why, *Why!* "

Entertaining though it was, the last straw was a north-eastern version of *House of the Rising Sun.*

"*There is a hooos in New-casss-illl, they caal the rye-ʒin' sun.*"

Sublime! I got out of bed, reached for my travel bag, rummaged for a pair of earplugs and stuffed one in each ear. Suddenly it sounded a whole lot better.

***

Dragons

The karaoke had long since finished when, at 6 o'clock, my alarm sounded and I rolled out of bed to see if the weather forecasters had been correct. They were partly correct. It was indeed cold and cloudy for July, very cold in fact, but they hadn't forecast the cloud to be so low that the Hotel and the bay were totally immersed in a thick grey soup. Visibility was less than 100 metres. Neither had they predicted the rain to be so heavy. I had only seen rain like this once before, on that day in June when dangerously flooded rivers cut off Chesterfield. It was as if the gods believed the North York Moors were on fire and were trying to put it out by draining the sea onto the land.

Looking west from the window I couldn't see the mast at the top of the hill. In fact, where was the hill? There was nothing but the grey soup and the bouncing rain. The previous concerns about sunburn couldn't have been more misguided. The sun had been doused out. My immediate thought was to get straight back in bed and do the run another day. But damn it, there wasn't another day. We were all here now, and it was only water anyway. Very cold, very wet, very watery, water.

"Get out there and do it, you big girl's blouse", encouraged Andrea. I thought about whether I would rather suffer the ordeals she went through or spend a day running in heavy rain. I decided not to be a big girl's blouse, and got out there to do it.

Mal and Justin were already in the hotel's breakfast area when I got there. The tables were deserted apart from my two colleagues. Breakfast didn't officially start for over an hour, but we had explained our early start to the waiters the evening before and they arranged for enough milk, cereals and juice to be available for us. There was also a steaming pot of coffee. Our breakfast was small and quickly eaten to ensure we got off to an early start as there was a long drive ahead to get to Osmotherley.

Andy arrived at his normal fashionably late time, just as we had finished eating. Mal and Justin chivvied him along as I returned upstairs to kiss Andrea and tell her we were leaving. She barely moved, and mumbled "Good luck, see you later", sounding almost begrudging, but this was because she had fallen back to sleep and was tucked up snugly against the rain that was now trying to hammer its way through the window.

Grabbing our bags the four of us ran through the deluge to Andy's car, only to find that there wasn't enough room for us all to sit in it. The back seats were covered in boxes and gadgets, food and drink. Two partly dismantled mountain bikes added to the mess. A few extra minutes were spent getting even wetter whilst we put the bikes on the roof rack and re-arranged pieces of this human-and-luggage jigsaw puzzle. With Mal in the passenger seat, myself behind him, Justin next to me, and paraphernalia filling every space in between, Andy started the engine and headed for the A171.

It took a long time to warm up in the car. The windows refused to de-mist, and any warm air blown from the heater was struggling to get around the numerous bags of jelly-sweets and biscuits that were piled up on the dashboard. I sat wishing I had put on more clothes for the journey. Several other drivers were travelling through the deluge, and every car that passed hissed up an angry spray of water behind it, giving the appearance that we were all in a powerboat race rather than a car journey.

The windscreen wipers were in overdrive. Like two boys starting a fight, they lunged across the windscreen faster and faster as if taking turns to push the other off the side of the car. Inside it was cramped and cold, and there was a long way to go to the start. This did little for my confidence. If I had to finish the run where the car journey started, and we were going to drive for two hours to get to the start of the run, how long would I have to run for? And it was bucketing it down. Bloody hell! This was madness.

I had my kit bag on my lap. In it were my usual long run essentials of Vaseline, nipple guards, spare clothes, and food and drinks. I decided to get as ready as I could in the car as we drove along. This was to prove an entertaining challenge considering the extremely limited space for movement combined with the speedy and swaying movements of the car as Andy launched it around the northern edge of the North York Moors. Firstly I applied nipple guards. This was a relatively simple task, albeit a cold one. All I had to do was lift the front of my jacket and t-shirt and stick them on.

Removing my shoes and socks and lathering Vaseline on my feet before reapplying the footwear was in a different league of challenging. I also had to attempt to smear Vaseline on my inner thighs, under my armpits and on my back and shoulders where my backpack would sit. By the time I had finished with the Vaseline we had driven about twenty miles and rounded a few hundred bends, and I most likely resembled a greased-up cross-channel swimmer. Added to that, the Vaseline in my shorts meant that I slid across the back seat every time the car went round a bend. Had we had a crash I would have slipped under my seat belt, slimed easily between the front seat and the car door, and oozed through the struggling dashboard air vents. There was so much Vaseline where it shouldn't have been that the car was probably leaving a trail like a giant snail all the way from Ravenscar to Osmotherley.

Andy switched on the radio. The news report informed us that the unprecedented heavy rain had hit most of the country. Whole towns had been isolated, water supplies contaminated, and power to tens of thousands of homes cut off as electricity stations disappeared underwater. Dams threatened to burst, and tragically, people had been killed. If ever there was a day for running an exposed hilltop ultra-marathon, this wasn't it.

The four of us were laughing and joking despite the foul, gloomy conditions. Or maybe we were laughing and joking *because* of the foul, gloomy conditions. Either way, the journey was entertaining, and very reminiscent of the times we had spent as a team on the coast-to-coast, although a big hole was left due to the absence of Vin.

Mal put the maps to one side for a moment and reached down into his kit bag. He pulled out a plastic tub containing a strange looking orange paste, and offered some to us all, asking, "Anyone want some cold orange porridge?"

"What?" we all replied, bemused.

"Cold orange porridge. You tip oats into a tub the evening before you need them, pour orange juice over them, put them in the fridge overnight, and in the morning you have orange porridge. But it's cold".

Silence from the other three of us.

"It's good endurance fuel. A little strange at first, but you might like it," he added. He pulled some dessert spoons from his kit bag and waved them in the air. Curiosity forced Justin take the tub from him and have a closer look. He sniffed the orangey goo; a big, hard sniff, and he suddenly turned into Jilly Goulding, the wine critic. "Hmmm, I'm getting a heavy aroma of oranges, with a subtle whiff of oats and, if I'm not mistaken, I can just detect a tang of Vaseline and cheap deodorant." All true, except that the Vaseline smell was from me, and the deodorant from Andy.

Justin took a spoon from Mal, scooped a lump out and ate it. We all watched his face, even Andy who was craning his neck to view using his rear-view mirror. Justin chewed, swallowed, and gave his opinion.

"Hmmm, I'm not sure," he announced in a slow and deliberate manner, looking pensive. We all watched intently as he took another spoonful. "Hmmmmmmm," he repeated.

"I know your game, you're nicking it all," I blurted. "Give it here."

I grabbed a spoon from Mal and took a tentative mouthful. It was certainly unusual, but not unpleasant, and not surprisingly had the taste of orange and the texture of cold porridge.

"Not too bad," was my assessment.

Andy declined the orange porridge, but the rest of us shared the tub. It was all eaten before we passed through Stokesley, on the A172.

For a brief moment the dark, high Cleveland Hills, eroded over millions of years from a huge slab of middle Jurassic rock, revealed themselves close to our left as a fissure of light squeezed weakly through a narrow chink in the armour of the heavy, grey cloud that was draped over the land. They looked ominous, as if revealing their full size, power and dominance, like a boxer psychologically willing his opponent into submission before the bell rings for the first round of the bout. I tried not to feel submissive, but there was a definite sensation of nervousness that threatened to overcome any excitement.

The hills undoubtedly have an imposing and mountainous characteristic, arising steeply and aggressively from the flat, calm vale that surrounds them. Early British inhabitants tended to live on the higher hills rather than struggle in the choking, strangling, thick forests that used to cover the valley. Folklore tells of stories about monsters and wild creatures that lived in the wilder retreats and the steep, narrow valleys of the high moors, and traditions abound of brave and courageous men who had slain terrible beasts that lived on the hills. Deforestation on the vale led to agriculture and the movement of settlements down from the higher ground. But the hills still purvey an ominous presence that whispers, "*There be dragons!*"

We turned off the main road at Swainby, and onto the small lane heading up Scugdale. I recognised it immediately, having dragged my knee pixie up there fourteen months earlier. The road climbed steeply, crossed a cattle grid, and descended more slowly towards the village of Osmotherley, which, it is suggested, is named after a clearing, or 'ley', belonging to a Viking named 'Asmund', or a Saxon called 'Osmund'. To give indication as to the age of the village, the name supposedly appeared in the Doomsday Book as 'Asmundrelac'.

Our destination was about a mile before and above the village, in a small car park on Scarth Wood Moor, adjacent to Cod Beck reservoir. The stream that fills the reservoir before flowing into the river Swale gets its name from the Celtic word 'Coed', meaning woody.

Andy drove the car into the deserted gravel car park and switched off the engine. The rain on the car roof sounded like a million marbles rolling down a wooden staircase. Down to our right we could see the reservoir.

The surface of the water looked like it was boiling under the deluge falling from the sky. So much rainwater was gushing down the road it looked like you could white-water raft into Osmotherley. The bracken on the hills all around was bent double under the force of the persistent precipitation. Sunburn, eh? I had sun cream in my kit bag, but it was as necessary as swimming trunks in the Sahara.

We all looked at each other and laughed, all thinking the same thing, 'If no one else gets out of the car, I'll stay here too'. Pride trumped sanity and I stepped outside dressed in my *winter* running gear, including hat and gloves. Mal and Justin both jumped out and, also wearing winter biking clothing, hurriedly began to remove their bikes from the roof rack. I was wet through before I had my CamelBak ready and on my back, and the wind was picking up, adding to the chill.

Suddenly and amazingly we weren't alone. Another car pulled into the car park, wet stones and gravel crunching crisply under its tyres. A middle-aged lady stepped out, pulled on a huge overcoat, strode to the back of her vehicle and opened the boot. Out leapt a huge dog which began bounding around excitedly, anticipating a walk on the hills. Both seemed oblivious to the torrent although the woman greeted us with, "Not a nice day today!"

We all naturally agreed. She asked us where we were heading.

"Ravenscar, we all said in unison.

"Good grief," she replied, "That's a long way. At least you have bikes."

"He hasn't, he's running," announced Justin and Mal, pointing at me.

"*To Ravenscar?*" she enquired, looking unbelieving.

"Er, yes," I answered sheepishly.

"Good grief! Good luck!"

And with that she bounded after her equally bounding dog, and disappeared into the sodden bracken.

Alone again we each did a final gear check, Andy clipped a radio on my chest strap, and the two bikers and I stood briefly for a photo while Orff's *Carmina Burana* blared out from the car stereo. Standing outside in that heavy rain any longer would have been a really, really silly thing to do. Totally stupid. So we set off for the hills.

The official start of the Lyke Wake walk is the old standing stone set in the ground on Scarth Wood Moor. The rain had clearly washed away part of our memories as we forgot to look for the stone. Had we cast a glance over the lane from the car park we would have seen it a few metres from the road.

The first short section of the route involved running back up the road we had driven along through Scarth Wood Moor. I was first away, pottering at a steady pace that I considered sustainable, each footstep slapping the wet road and splashing water up my shins. After a minute I heard Mal and Justin chatting behind me, and the three of us reached the brow of the hill at the same time. The cloud had dropped even further, and we were now shrouded in sodden gloom and unable to see more than 50 metres. On a normal day the view would stretch for many miles towards the city of Middlesborough on the North East coast.

A glance at the map informed me I had to look for a track off into the woods on the right, just past the cattle grid. The bikers found the track first and held the gate open for me to pass through. I had run less than a mile on tarmac. There would be no more road running for another twenty miles.

The gravel track took us into a wooded section through Clain Wood. This was to be the only sheltered stretch of the whole run, and it resembled a tropical rainforest. But cold!

Low, thick cloud stuck in the trees like smoke, and the dense foliage drooping from sodden branches gathered raindrops into huge blobs before dropping them like water bombs. But at least we were out of the wind. The trail dropped steeply down a stepped path to the first of three 'Round Hills' on the route before turning right up Scugdale, and meandering and undulating for a kilometre like a slimy roller coaster. Out of the wind I was rapidly warming up. I was ahead of the two bikers at this point but soon had to step to the side to let Mal pass on a gentle uphill section. His back wheel spun and slid sideways as the tyre fought for traction on the wet, slippery, muddy trail. But where was Justin? It was surely too soon for him to be to be struggling.

I was beginning to feel too warm by the time I reached a gate where the path cut left and descended through a field, leading to the stream, Scugdale Beck, that ran down the valley. Mal held the gate open for me, and also for Justin who arrived there as I did. My newfound warmth, in addition to being temporarily sheltered from the wind, caused me to worry about overheating so early on such a long run. I was wet, very wet in fact, but the exercise had warmed the water next to my skin. I decided to take a few moments by the gate to remove my leggings, jacket, hat and gloves, and stuffed them into my backpack.

Thankfully I would live to regret this foolishness.

***

In the Wake of the Dead

Justin and Mal had ridden down the field and were out of sight before I set off running again. Scugdale Beck was in flood, but fortunately there was a high wooden bridge that enabled my safe crossing. On the other side of the stream a farm track twisted steeply upwards to the road that wound its way up the valley. I walked this steep track, conserving energy. On reaching the road I recognised it as the one that had tortured my left knee during the coast-to-coast. Looking to the right I could see the place where I stopped to text Phil the Pill for pharmacological advice. Standing at almost the same spot were my biking friends who were studying the map. I shouted and waved farewell to them, as we were going separate ways for the next fifteen miles.

I crossed the road straight onto a small footpath that headed upwards to the unseen heavens past Live Moor Plantation and Knolls End, and towards the second 'Round Hill'. The path was mostly covered in an inch of running water. Initially it wasn't too steep, and I ran slowly, but the gradient soon increased in brutality and I was forced to walk again. At a narrow wooden gate the path took a sharp right turn, and headed very steeply on stone steps set in the soil, straight up the hill through mature deciduous woodland.

The gate swung closed behind me with a satisfying wooden smack, and I pushed on. This was hard going. The stone surface was slippery, the gradient severe, and my breathing was heavy and noisy. I sounded like a miniature version of the hissing cacophony that was produced above me as the sodden, high leaf canopy waved and danced violently in windy gusts. Overhead, the boughs shook ominously, as if danced upon by a coven of cackling witches. Every swing and shake of the branches caused more watery bombardment.

I was trying to maintain a sustainable pace and keep my breathing in check as I reached another gate at the top of the woodland. Through this one I could see the stone path leading further skyward into the cloud. The top was still not visible. I continued with a fast walking speed, and as I rose above the tree line I stepped into nature's jet-wash. There was no protection from the elements. The wind blasted hard and the rain scythed horizontally and relentlessly. Still, no reason to stop, I thought, pressing onwards.

On two or three occasions throughout the climb I slowed to check the map. I was still ascending towards an unseen summit, and whilst I was reasonably sure I was on the correct trail the last thing I wanted was to run up the wrong hill. Staring at the chart I noticed the word *tumulus* written in small letters. Then I saw another one nearby, and another. Once focused on them, it was clear that there were hundreds of tumuli marked on the map: hundreds and hundreds of ancient burial sites.

The dead were all around, scattered all over the hills, surrounding me. I was going higher and higher, while the wind whistled wildly, buffeting and hissing in my ears like a circling gaggle of ghosts, taking turns to dive close to me, scream and spit, and then whirl away skywards. "*Fool, fool, fool*" they whispered, then "*Dragons! There be dragons*", then "*Go home, home, home*". The heather and short, stubborn grass trembled and vibrated, shaking its fist as if rattled by angered subterranean spirits, shouting "*Leave the moor, leave the moor*".

My core temperature was still comfortable, or so I thought, but feeling a trickle of cold water run down my back prompted me to re-assess the situation. The rain was blasting the left side of my face, and this was becoming numb. Yet my bare legs felt nothing. Alarm bells started to ring in my mind. I reached down with my hand and touched my thigh. The skin felt icy cold and lifeless. More worryingly, both hand and thigh were numb.

I was in a very dangerous situation. Wind and rain together are the cause of many hypothermia casualties, and I had foolishly put myself at risk. Body heat vaporises any water next to the skin, and moving air blows this vapour away, taking the heat with it. This is what happens when we sweat, which is a mechanism used to cool the body. Lots of cold rainwater in combination with a strong wind has a severe and rapid cooling effect.

The hypothalamus (a small portion of the brain that is located just above the brain stem) plays a vital role in controlling body temperature. In fact, for such a small lump of tissue, it performs an astonishing number of the body's vital housekeeping chores. The primary function of the hypothalamus is 'homeostasis', or maintaining the body's status quo. As well as keeping body temperature at a steady level it also regulates (among other things) blood pressure, fluid and electrolyte balance, digestion, heart rate, sweating, adrenaline levels and body weight. To do this, the hypothalamus receives signals about the state of the body, and can make compensatory changes if anything is out of normal range.

I had read about several deaths from hypothermia, where all the victims had significant mountain experience and should not have been caught out so badly, even in the poor weather to which they were exposed. There seemed to be a common theme to the deaths; the victims were alone and the bodies were eventually found wearing only light clothing, their cold weather clothing and waterproofs either stuffed in their rucksack or scattered around them as if they had made no attempt to keep warm.

It is believed that each casualty had been travelling quickly and was producing a lot of heat from their muscles. This had warmed their core temperature. However, the combined effects of wind and rain had caused rapid cooling of the limbs. What is assumed is that the hypothalamus was receiving mixed signals, and it is believed that a state of warm core temperature with cool and rapidly chilling extremities can confuse the thermal regulation response.

Combined with elements of fatigue and possibly low blood sugar and fluctuating electrolyte levels (due to the exercise) the hypothalamus malfunctioned, sending a message that the unfortunate person was too hot. They then started to remove clothing when they should be putting more on, worsening the cycle of heat loss and spiralling into hypothermia and the mental confusion that goes with it. Without immediate rescue from the elements causing the situation, death would be inevitable.

My core temperature was warm, but my limbs were cold and cooling. Fortunately I wasn't yet fatigued, and still had the mental capacity to be able to get myself out of trouble. I stopped immediately, took my leggings, jacket, hat and gloves out of my pack and put them straight on. The next two essential things to do were to get warmer and get somewhere else. The only way to achieve both objectives was to get running again. I checked the map. With such poor visibility I had little to go on. I was climbing a hill. According to my compass I was going in an east-north-easterly direction, and the slope fell away to my left. All three things were consistent with where I believed myself to be, so I increased the pace to get my muscles to produce more heat and act as a central heating boiler for my chilled limbs.

My heart beat faster and the pumped blood carried warmth to the areas it was most needed. Within a couple of minutes I realised I had done the right thing and had avoided potential disaster. I was feeling warmer, happier and mentally more alert. The ghosts still circled noisily overhead, but no longer swooped low or screamed in my ears. It scared me to think how easily I had allowed myself to make a simple error that quickly dragged me into danger. Sunburn! I'd narrowly escaped hypothermia.

Much as I love being on the hills in pretty much all conditions I was beginning to wish I had stayed in bed after all. This weather could be far better appreciated from behind the defences of a double-glazed window, curtains and a warm duvet. Andrea would just be getting up about now, enjoying a cup of tea in bed before heading down to the hotel restaurant for a relaxing and hearty breakfast with the other Andrea. Sudden contemplation of the relative merits of fresh coffee and Full English, or force-10 and freezing rain, brought the conclusion that this was indeed madness.

I passed under the brow of Round Hill (the second), still running, and on thousands of large slabs of stone set carefully into the path. I believed myself to be on the Cleveland Way, a very popular long distance footpath that all but circumnavigates the vast expanse of the North York Moors. The stones had recently been placed to aid footpath conservation and prevent erosion of the soft moorland terrain, a problem often encountered where many pairs of boots roam the wild and beautiful hills.

Opened in 1969, The Cleveland Way was the second National Trail in England and Wales, and stretches for 110 miles (177Km), starting at the cross in the Market Square in Helmsley before half encircling the largest open moorland in England and striking the Yorkshire coast at Saltburn. It then follows the coastal path southwards, through Staithes, Whitby, Robin Hood's Bay and Scarborough, before ending at Filey Brigg.

The official website of the Cleveland Way states that "... there is a wealth of history and heritage to enjoy. Helmsley Castle, Rievaulx Abbey, Mount Grace Priory, Gisborough Priory, Whitby Abbey and Scarborough Castle to name just a few special sites", and that "An invigorating walk on any part of the route is the ultimate stress beater". Today it was me that was being given a beating, not my stress.

The stones in the ground acted as a very useful guide. However as I could see little farther than the stones in the ground I once again checked the compass to ensure I was heading in the correct direction. The wind was still strong but mercifully the rain was easing slightly. I was extremely thankful for the plastic map case I was using. If the map had not been protected, it would have been shredded by the gale and scattered across the moors like soggy confetti.

After rounding the northern edge of Gold Hill I was able to jog at a reasonable pace along Faceby Bank, although I couldn't get rid of the nagging doubts that I may be running wildly in a random direction into the fog. The map indicated there should be a gliding club, 200-metres to my right. That was more than four times further than I could see. For all I knew there could have been *Elvis* riding a *unicorn* around *Atlantis* 200-metres to my right!

I ran with care through the gloom as the map was showing there to be crags close by on my left side. Avoiding hypothermia only to run off a cliff wouldn't be good. To my right side stood damp, desolate moorland that could have stretched a hundred miles or a hundred metres, I really had no idea. My progress wasn't fast due to the regular navigation checks, but it was steady, and before long I found myself bounding carefully down a steep, slippery slope through a disused quarry that should take me to the first meeting point with Andy at a lane above Carlton Bank.

I found my way down the winding path through the grey darkness to the checkpoint where Andy was indeed waiting. I'd covered the first six miles in 50-minutes – faster than I had thought. The car boot was open, and next to it laid Andy's portable stove with a kettle on top. He offered me some food and a cup of tea, but told me he'd had trouble finding the checkpoint due to the weather and as a result the stove had just been switched on. It would take a while for the kettle to boil. I declined the offer as I still had enough food and drink in my backpack to get to checkpoint two. Helpful as ever though, he offered me some orange-tinted light-enhancing sunglasses. The visibility was so bad there was definitely no harm in trying them. I thanked him for them, said I'd see him at the next checkpoint, wished him a safe drive and ran across the lane to start the second leg.

I put the orange glasses on and suddenly everything had been *'Tango'd'*. I ran onwards through the murkiness, but at least with the glasses on it was a pleasing, tangerine, psychedelic kind of murkiness. With the compass out once again I headed for Cringle Moor, which should have been straight in front of me. But wasn't!

I found myself in a strange grassy landscape that stretched further than visibility in all directions. The grass had been cut short in strips that looked like paths, which headed in various directions, criss-crossing the area. This was confusing and I had no idea which one to run along. In the end I gave up following them and instead used the steep slope that plunged northwards off the hill and down into the valley as a guide. With this on my left Cringle Moor should have been directly in front of me. But still wasn't!

I had unwittingly started along on an alternative route round the north side of Cringle Moor, and only realised I'd missed the mountain when visibility briefly lifted to 80 metres or so and a big tango-orange hillside revealed itself towering upwards on my right. Bugger!

But never mind. I carried on running on a pleasant undulating bridleway that would have been fun to mountain bike along, and eventually re-found the Cleveland Way as it dropped off the east side of the hill. Cringle Moor had been circumnavigated rather than conquered.

The path descended into a small gulley before passing through a wall and immediately heading steeply upwards once again, towards the summit of a particularly pointy hill that is the northern point of Cold Moor. This was only a short, sharp climb, ascending a further 270 vertical feet, but it was very steep. Running wasn't an option, and even walking was tough going as my feet regularly slipped on the fierce slope.

I had to maintain energy levels and keep hydrated. I had watermelon flavour sports drink in my CamelBak, and this was beginning to have an unpleasant sickly sweetness to it. As well as drinking I pulled an energy bar from my pack, ripped it open and stuffed the wrapper into a pocket.

As I ground my way to the top of the hill, munching on the chewy bar, I wondered how the bikers were getting on in the wet and dark. Plucking the radio Andy had given me from the backpack chest strap, I pushed in the 'call' button and spoke.

"Mal, J, are you there"?

There was a lot of crackling, and mixed in with it were some difficult to hear voices that were broken and hissy, and appeared to be trying to hold a conversation. This didn't sound like Mal and Justin. More like a bad recording of Norman Collier's stand-up act duelling with Stephen Hawking suffering from a bad (computer) virus. I tried again, but there was still no sensible reply by the time I got to the summit. I re-clipped the radio safely on the chest strap for the plunge down the other side.

This descent was an exciting but tricky one, equally steep and slippery as the ascent. Before starting the run I was hopeful to make up any time lost on slow climbs by running hard and taking a few risks on the downs. This was, after all, how my hill training had been centred, but it was proving impossible. The dramatic lack of visibility coupled with the torrential rainfall simply made it far too dangerous. I was slipping and stumbling and nearly crashed headlong down the hill several times. So much for sunburn! So far I'd risked hypothermia, running off a crag and broken bones due to a nasty fall.

At the bottom of the hill, at a place called Garfit Gap, there were signs of life. A human figure dressed in heavy waterproofs and wearing a wide-brimmed green hat stood motionless in the wet murkiness, looking like a scarecrow taking a nocturnal shower and not particularly enjoying it. The man said nothing, but tipped his head in a subtle, almost imperceptible, nod of recognition as I sped by. I'm sure we were both thinking much the same thing – what the hell is that idiot doing up here in this weather? It was a very hard question to answer. With hindsight, he was probably thinking "What the hell is that idiot doing up here in this weather *wearing orange sunglasses?*"

My legs were starting to feel the first sensations of fatigue due to the incessant steep climbing and descending. So far there had been precious little flat ground on which I could actually run in a sensible and comfortable rhythm. And when I *could* run my feet were slipping and sliding in all directions on the mud and wet stones. This hammered the muscles around my hips and abdomen, the muscles that battle to keep me upright and moving in the right direction. With less than ten miles covered it was dawning on me that this was indeed going to be a long and arduous journey.

This seemed to be the only dawning, as on the next steep climb up Hasty Bank night came. Or so I thought.

It had become so dark that even with the *Tango*'s on I was convinced I had started the run at 8.45 pm instead of 8.45 am. I took off the glasses. They were covered in rain anyway, making visibility no better than without them. The saw-tooth profile to the run continued as this was yet another thigh-burning, energy-sapping and steep climb.

Hasty Bank wears a crown of huge rocks called the Wain Stones, angular and leaning, which to me had the appearance of fallen castle battlements. The path winds between them, splitting into tiny tributaries that try and pick the best way through, up and around the imposing and domineering slabs that slant and tower over like giants. But there is no 'best' way, only several very difficult ways.

Apparently the stones give the impression of a wagon, or 'wain', on the hilltop, hence the name. I couldn't see the wagon. I could only see grey, wet, daunting Jurassic monsters looming above me. I did my best to keep moving before I was slain by them. Then a miracle happened.

As quick as flipping a switch, the lights turned on and the world came out to play. A huge gap in the clouds opened up to my left, revealing a staggeringly beautiful view down into the valley a thousand feet below. I could see for miles. It was as if the gods had thrust a sword through the fabric of the sky and used it to stir up the stratosphere. Shafts of sunlight cut through expanding gaps in the cloud like sabres slicing cotton wool, casting spot-light bright areas on the valley bottom that raced each other across the land as the wind swept rapidly onwards. And there were houses down there too, and cars driving along roads like lines of ants on tree branches. This lifted my spirits considerably. I felt alive, strong, and optimistic about getting to the end of the run

With renewed energy I started bounding down a smooth and solid path towards the B1257 road above Clay Bank, which was where Andy should be waiting at checkpoint 2. Despite being a few hundred yards away I could clearly see the road, but not the red *'Respect The Stupidity'* support car. I called on the radio.

"Andy, are you there?"

"Wey-heyy! I'm here, checkpoint two. Where are you?" came the instant reply. How things had changed. As well as the sunlight we now had radio communication rather than just crackly ghostly voices mumbling unintelligible babble. I had been struggling through a cold, dark and frightening place, only to be cast joyously out into the light of a beautiful world. Was I being given a 'true' Lyke Wake experience? Was this how it was for the spirits of the dead as they made their last laborious and soulful passage across the moors from the mortal world before stepping into the afterlife?

The Blue Man

I stumbled onto the road to find Andy standing by the car. Once again the boot was open revealing his mobile delicatessen. A cup of tea was waiting for me, gently steaming in a comforting manner. Andy recharged the drink in my CamelBak with more watermelon goo while I sipped the tea and stuffed in mouthfuls of his homemade flapjack, made to his 'special' recipe to contain vast quantities of energy. It was known as *Jacked-Up*, and was delicious. As we stood describing our relative ordeals of the last two hours, a woman approached and asked if I had seen a Jack Russell dog on the hills. I apologised and said I hadn't.

A Jack Russell dog? I hadn't even seen the bloody hills!

As I stuffed the flapjack into my very grateful mouth I asked Andy if he had heard from the two cyclists. He hadn't, but was expecting to see them at the next checkpoint. That would also be my next rendezvous with him, and at a location we'd used on the coast-to-coast. I set off running again, and heard Andy re-arranging his goods into the car boot before starting the engine and setting off.

I was back to walking pace almost immediately on a steep track onto Carr Ridge, still following the Cleveland Way and heading for the third 'Round Hill'. This one was familiar to me. It was the brow to which I was bearing on our last big adventure when my left knee collapsed and I was forced to resort to pharmacological assistance. On that occasion the weather was cold and drizzly, where as now it was, well, cold but not currently raining. The stubborn cloud was doing its very best to smear in front of the few small wisps of blue sky.

As the gradient lessened I was able to jog again, and in front of me and half to the left revealed a spectacular and striking view of the cliffs rising and curving sharply northwards around Greenhow Moor. The harsh magnificence of the North York Moors and its sudden and dramatic explosion from the flat vale around it was impressively increased by the contrasts blowing swiftly through the sky above. Shades of blue and grey marched onwards while laser beams of sunlight pierced through, and brown moorland beginning its first chameleon-like turn to purple proudly presented itself above tree-covered hillsides. At the top of the banks, crags and bare rocky outcrops looked angrily down into the vale, some glistening where sun shone on their rain-soaked surface, like warriors waving their shields at oncoming attackers. It was true rugged beauty.

And I could also see other people. It wasn't just myself and the Garfit Gap scarecrow who had been foolish enough to run to the hills. Small clusters of walkers could be seen spread over the wide area of moorland that was now visible. Some were a few hundred yards ahead on the trail I was taking up Urra Moor. Farther to the right were other walkers making their way along the wide track that headed from Seave Green to Cockayne Head. In my mind I could still visualise clearly that particular track as it was in May 2006, teasing and taunting me to run up it when I could barely walk.

In fact there were so many small groups of people on the hills it now looked like a normal Saturday rather than moorland meteorological Armageddon. The track from Seave Green joined the highest point of the Cleveland Way at the top of Round Hill, and from here I was on familiar terrain, knowing that I'd be able to maintain a good pace for at least the next four miles.

A slight descent and a hop over a small stream led to the disused railway line at Bloworth Crossing. I now had an easy section of flat, smooth cinder track on a trail that wound its way in a sinusoidal manner around the top of four small stream gulleys towards The Lion Inn and Blakey Ridge.

The railway track, now devoid of rails and sleepers, once covered over ten miles of bleak moorland to Rosedale. It was initially established in 1858 by the North Eastern Railway Company to transfer ironstone mined by The Rosedale Ironstone Mining Company to Ferryhill Ironworks. The work was dangerous, and accidents on the line were common. Trade in calcine dust briefly extended operations, but all traffic ceased by 1929 and the line was closed. Railway workers cottages were built at the bottom and the top of the incline to the moor. The settlement at the top became known as 'Siberia' by the workers, due to the regular treacherous weather conditions.

I quickly got into a good running rhythm, and there was a pleasing crunch from the cinders with every step. Finally able to maintain a steady rate of effort my temperature rose above comfortable level, and I removed my windproof jacket for the second time, but fear of repeating the previous mistake prevented me taking anything else off. I pulled out my radio and called to Mal and Justin, convinced they would be on the railway line ahead of me. There was still no answer.

This was certainly the easiest running of the entire route, and good speed was maintained all the way to the tiny black dotted line on the map that cut eastwards across the moor from the railway line to Rosedale Head. This was 'Jackson's Path', a very small trail that sneaked through the heather moorland. I had used Jackson's Path on the penultimate day of the coast-to-coast, and remembered the point where it met the old railway line. Jumping the ditch that ran adjacent to the cinder track, I immediately found myself in a swampy peat bog, through which flowed not Jackson's Path but Jackson's *River*. The whole moor was completely saturated from the torrential rainfall. Huge quantities of water were pouring down through the heather. There was no way of avoiding another soaking.

Although mostly narrow, the path occasionally widened where boots and the elements had eroded the peat. Today the wide sections were lakes of standing water, separated by streams down which the water flowed and bubbled. There was no point in trying to keep dry. I simply had to ignore the conditions and follow the underwater path, even though I was wading knee deep at times. The moorland rose steadily in front of me for a mile. I was going up the creek without a paddle.

I tried again to call the bikers, thinking the extra height might enable a stronger radio signal. This time I had success. Mal returned my call within seconds. I asked where they were, expecting them to have comfortably beaten me to the next rendezvous. I was surprised when he said they were just approaching the railway line, and the tone of his voice suggested he wasn't pleased. He explained that Justin was struggling and that progress was very slow.

Jackson's path-cum-river led out onto the road north of the Lion Inn. I could see the crew car waiting for me in a lay-by a mile ahead. I had a choice of staying on the small road that curved around the head of the valley, or taking a shorter straight line along a soggy bridleway that dipped down to a stream gulley before climbing to the lay-by. I chose to stay off-road.

Ahead were four walkers, all wearing heavy waterproofs and sporting waterproof covers over their rucksacks. They reached the crew car, and I could see Andy chatting to them. He took a couple of photos as I approached, but missed the action shot of me losing my footing and diving facedown in the mud close to the road. The walkers had continued along a path heading northeastwards. I was tired and was looking forward to sitting in the car for a few minutes to warm up, and longed to change into dry clothes.

Andy spoke of his conversation with the walkers, who were all young men, and who were walking the Lyke Wake route. They had set off the previous day and spent the night at the Lion Inn. Andy had told them that I was also attempting the Lyke Wake, and had set off at eight-o-clock. They thought he was talking about eight-o-clock the previous day, and couldn't believe that I had made it this far in one morning. I replied that it was no surprise that they were taking much longer over the walk – they had just gone along the wrong path, in entirely the wrong direction.

As he plied me with tea and biscuits I piled on more clothes. The cold had ground into me much deeper than I had realised and I sat for half an hour trying to de-frost. It frightened me to think that hypothermia could strike so easily in the middle of summer.

I peeled off my sodden, mud-stained shoes and socks to reveal feet I didn't recognise. They looked mummified after having been immersed in a cold dirty bath for the last few hours. They were so wrinkled and grimy that the toes resembled a collection of dried prunes. I could well have imagined what trench foot must look and smell like. Socks were changed for dry ones and feet were wiped and re-coated in Vaseline.

Andy's phone rang. It was Vin enquiring how things were going. The phone was passed to me and Vin was surprised to hear my voice. His initial thoughts were that I'd had to abandon the effort, and he was relieved to hear that I was simply having a pit stop. He wished me well, and I prepared to set off for the next leg. By now the rain looked to have gone for the day and the few small breaks in the clouds seemed to be increasing, although the wind was still stiff and cold.

As I laced up my shoes in preparation to leave Mal rode into view on the road near the Inn. It was clearly difficult on the bike, and he was struggling to make headway up the slope into the wind. There was no sign of Justin. It took nearly ten minutes for Mal to make the mile journey to the car. When he arrived he was very cold, hungry and covered in mud. It was obvious that the bike trails were in as sloppy a state as the paths – conditions that sap the energy of riders. He was feeling surprisingly good but said that Justin was finding it an ordeal and had been going really slowly from the start.

As Mal climbed off his bike Justin appeared on the far horizon. He was moving much slower than Mal had been. Then it became clear that he was not moving at all. He had ground to a halt on the slight incline. Happy that the bikers were both safe and in the hands of Andy, I decided I needed to keep moving and set off to find the path across Rosedale Moor towards checkpoint four

So far I'd run for four hours and covered about 22 miles – half way. Justin, on the other hand, was coming to the end of his adventure. A lack of training for the last year was taking its toll. The ride would have been a tough one for a fit rider. Attempting it from a base fitness of ground-level was ambitious to say the least. But attempt it he did and, credit where credit is due, he tried hard and rode himself into the ground. When he eventually dragged himself and his bike through the wind and around the road to the crew car he decided he'd had enough (actually I think he decided he'd had enough a long way before then).

Mal and Andy were relieved. If Justin had expressed any desire to continue they would have shown him the 'red card' and told him to stay in the car. There was no way he would have made it to the end, and he was holding Mal back, threatening his success. As the saying goes, 'Fail to prepare and you prepare to fail'. Since this incident Justin has become a cult figure within the team for his "It'll be all right" attitude of that day - so much so that an entire training ethos has arisen around him. It is known as *J-Training*. J-training involves doing no training whatsoever. It is the easiest training program ever devised, and therein lays its only benefit.

Along the road from the checkpoint came a junction. The last time I ran here I turned left and headed north to Glaisdale. Today I took the right fork before turning left, due east, along a track described on the map as a boundary, which carried on for nearly four miles across the open moor. In preparing for the run I had been concerned that this might be small and difficult to follow. In fact it was a sizeable trench gouged through the peat by the passage of thousands of walkers. It was poker-straight and almost flat, barring minor undulations.

With the rain gone and visibility rapidly improving, getting lost would have been hard to do. Unfortunately, moving at a reasonable pace was also hard to do. So much rain had fallen that I could probably have swum across the moor and turned the event into a duathlon. Everywhere was bog, swamp and mire.

The trench-path was three-to-four feet deep at first, with vertical peat walls and a foot-thick layer of wet bog in the bottom. It was virtually impossible to run. I tried clambering out and running through the heather at the rim of the trench. This was almost as difficult. The heather was knee deep and grew in humps that threatened falls and twisted ankles. Every twenty yards or so a stream gulley cut sideways into the trench, requiring me either to drop down and clamber up the other side, or go a long way round it. Progress was slow, but I chose to keep out of the trench.

Matt Beardshall

I rapidly caught up with another group of walkers who were having similar difficulties but who had opted for the trench. There were four or five of them, all covered in mud up to their knees, and all concentrating on keeping upright. I jogged through the heather above and to their right. A middle-aged chap looked at me as I passed and exclaimed, "Oh, well done." I had the feeling that they too had accepted the Lyke Wake challenge.

The path dropped downwards and opened out into a ludicrously wide marsh. Clumps of straight, thin reeds fan-tailed upwards, interspersed within a dense green carpet of mossy, carpet-like vegetation that did its best to cling to the surface of a sloppy, black quagmire. Boot prints spread out in all directions where walkers had come to the swamp and attempted to find a way round. In some places the prints just vanished as if the unfortunate victim had sunk without trace. That couldn't be excluded as a possibility, but I preferred to hope that the prints had disappeared as the fluid ground oozed back to a level surface.

I halted for a moment to weigh up my options. There appeared to be no sensible way across to the left. No sensible way across to the right. No sensible way straight across. No sensible way!

Sense therefore floundered around wondering what to do, and bravado took over, grabbed the controls and accelerated me in a straight line towards what appeared to be the out-path on the other side of the swamp a hundred yards ahead. Bravado had a plan. If I went fast and tried to 'bounce' my feet off the surface I might get across unscathed, especially if I used some of the reeds like stepping-stones. Bravado had been watching nature programs on television, and wanted me to be like one of those lizards that run on water. Bravado was an idiot!

I made four steps before a foot went under, my momentum ceased, and the other leg slopped up to knee level in thick, black, oozing, foul-smelling bog. Both arms instinctively stretched outwards as I fell forward, and I just managed to stop myself with some reeds before diving headlong into the fetid mire. What surprised me wasn't sinking in the peat, this was clearly inevitable. What surprised me was how much effort it took to extract myself and get moving again. And there was just no way of telling where the ground would take my weight and where I'd sink in putrid quicksand-like mud.

There really was no point in trying to find any way other than a straight line. Maintaining forward momentum required constant high effort. Briefly I stood on what appeared solid ground, and took a few seconds rest. I reached for my radio to call the team and tell them of the conditions, but the radio was gone. Damn!

It must have fallen unnoticed from my chest strap when I fell forward. The radio belonged to Andy. I didn't feel able to leave it, so there was only one thing to do. I turned back and attempted to re-trace my steps into the bog to find it. Although having been there only moments earlier it was impossible to see where I had been, the moor had swallowed any trace of my passing. I really had no idea where I had fallen and no idea where the radio could be. I assumed it had slowly made an oozing descent to the bottom of the mire. I thought that if I stayed there much longer the same would happen to me.

The group of walkers I'd passed had exited the ditch and were surveying the bog. Aware that I had almost zero chance of finding Andy's radio, and that I probably looked like a crazy mud-loving lunatic as I splattered aimlessly around in the slop, I abandoned my search and endeavoured to reach the other side before I sank and fossilized.

The bog gradually narrowed back into a muddy ditch at the other side. This was almost as impassable as the previous section, but had one difference. The vast rainfall had turned the bottom of the ditch into a stream, with the water flowing down into the bog now behind me. In places the water was just a couple of inches in depth, but in others it exceeded a foot.

I initially tried to avoid the water, instead ploughing a sticky furrow through the peat. But this was a pointless exercise as I was already soaking wet. I soon discovered that the best place to run was where the water was flowing as this was generally on a slightly more solid base, but this tactic involved taking a permanent cold shower as every step splashed water up my chest and into my face.

Traction on the slippery surface was at a premium, and I cursed my choice of footwear. The trail-running shoes were doing their best, but I began to think that my studded fell shoes would have fared better. However, some of the marks in the mud showed that aggressive-soled walking boots had also lost any kind of grip, and caused the wearers to skid in all directions. It was a battle that the mire was always going to win.

I tried to maintain momentum but every time a foot sank in the mud I'd get sudden painful cramp in one calf and then cramp in the opposite thigh as I tried quickly to extract the stuck limb. The ground constantly tried to suck the shoes off my feet. My legs were taking a real beating, stiffening and cramping, and constantly aching. If I kept to a steady rhythm they didn't hurt too much, but any rhythm was quickly broken with another foot sinking and sticking in the quagmire.

Boggy streams still cut across the path every few metres, forcing me again to make a decision on going round or ploughing through the middle. There was no way of knowing which way was better. I don't think either was better. The required effort was immense. I had run a marathon distance already, and now it was like trying to run another one wearing lead shoes and dragging a tyre. Running on the moors was usually heaven, but this was something different. It was beyond tough and challenging, this was a run like hell.

The Lyke Wake seemed cruel and relentless. I had crossed numerous moors already, gone over several horizons, and still the hills rolled away for miles in front of me, miles of heather, bog, rivers and steep climbs and descents. I wondered if the souls of the dead ever made it to heaven or if I would find them all resting in the next gulley, having given up the ghost (forgive the pun).

Very gradually the thick muddy section subsided and was replaced by a path that rose onto higher ground and was much firmer underfoot. It was still a stream, however, and the cold shower continued all the way to a tumulus called Shunner Howe. This was visible as a barrow standing on the hilltop, roughly a hundred feet across and ten feet high.

According to ancient folklore, the Howe was the home of a fairy creature by the name of T'Hob o' Shunner Howe. The Hob didn't appear to be home as I trundled by. To live in that barrow it must have been quite a small creature, and I imagined something like Tolkein's Hobbits. The names were so similar I thought they must have derived from the same source. However, this wasn't Middle Earth. It was beginning to feel more like the *end* of the Earth!

From the brow I had great views to the East, and could see Fylingdales Moor, still over ten miles away as the crow flies. (How I wished *I* could fly.)

Fylingdales is two contrasting worlds. A huge, grey, square concrete monstrosity, which houses a British Royal Air Force radar station, sits on top of a conservation area that covers 6,800 acres. The radar base is part of intelligence sharing arrangements between the United Kingdom and the United States, with the main purpose of giving warning of an impending missile attack, although it is also used to track orbiting objects.

The conservation area creates a nationally important haven for wildlife and archaeology. A fire on the moor in September 2003 destroyed an area of peat, which had accumulated over the centuries since farmers abandoned it for unknown reasons around 1000 years BC. This fire revealed hundreds of archaeologically important artefacts that provided remarkable insight into Stone Age and Bronze Age usage of the land. Modern and ancient, wild nature and a concrete carbuncle; Fylingdales is both beauty and the beast.

I splashed through the final few puddles of the track and strode onto the tarmac at checkpoint four on the road between Glaisdale and Rosedale. To my surprise the two Andreas were there, and they greeted me with a cheery hello and tales of a relaxing lay-in in warm and comfortable beds, followed by a slap-up breakfast and a good sit-down. Was I jealous? Hell, yes!

Also there were Andy and Justin, the latter appearing to be in need of a warm, comfortable bed. He looked exhausted and glad to be off the bike, which was fastened upright on the roof of the crew car. It was filthy, splattered with miles of riding and pushing through sloppy mud - mud that also clung in drying chunks on Justin's face where it had been thrown up by his front wheel.

All four of them were holding steaming cups of tea. I struggled to hold a conversation. I had been trying to drink my sports drink as often as possible throughout the run so far. The sickly flavour had been lovely for the first hour, but now it just made me gag. This wasn't good as it prevented me from drinking. Without increasing lost fluid a worsening state of dehydration would be inevitable.

Parked on the other side of the road was an estate car containing two people who kept looking back up the trail down which I had just run. I suspected they might have been a support crew for the walkers I had passed a few miles back. I hoped they had all made it across the bog.

I apologised to Andy about losing his radio. He didn't seem to mind too much, especially when I recounted the efforts I made trying to find it. A substitute radio was plucked from the car and clipped onto my pack. The effort involved in standing and trying to chat to the others made me feel sick and a little dizzy, so I decided not to stop long. An apple and a drink of water amounted to my total intake before starting towards the next path across White Moor.

The next trail was not unlike the previous one in that it was mostly a stream with numerous boggy sections that sucked my shoes off and cramped my calf and thigh muscles. I was heading towards a standing stone known as 'The Blue Man-i'-th'-Moss', reputedly the largest standing stone on the North York Moors.

This sounded particularly mysterious, almost spiritual, and I wasn't sure what to expect when I got there. In actual fact the name is thought to originate from either the Cornish words 'plyw', meaning parish, and 'men', meaning stone, or the Welsh 'plu', meaning parish, an 'maen', meaning stone. Either way it is simply a 'parish stone', but one that likely dates back to around the year 700 AD. A walking guide suggests that a visit to the Blue Man usually means one thing – getting wet.

After a mile the path petered out into smaller trails that were little more than rocky fissures winding through the heather moorland. I had been staggering along it for some time with nothing to see but the heather. Suddenly, there he was, the Blue Man, a few feet in front of me; a slightly rounded and weather-beaten stone, four or five feet high and a couple of feet wide, creamy white, and just *standing*.

On his south face someone had painted a small, blue man. There was something spiritual about him, something timeless, a domineering presence. He saw and knew everything that happened here. This was *his* moor. I said hello to him as I passed, but I don't think he liked me as he hid the path. Tiny trails meandered in all directions before petering out to nothingness. As a result I spent the next half hour stumbling and falling through thigh-deep heather, trying to beat my own path towards the tiny track that was shown on the map following the steep sides of Wheeldale Gill.

The heather was just beginning to display its earliest blooms of summer colour. Given another month it would be beautifully and proudly presenting its vivid purple, making the entire moor and the hills stunning from miles around. And rare! Three quarters of the world's heather moorland is found in Britain, of which the North York Moors is a huge expanse. Not only are the moorlands themselves rare but they are vital feeding and breeding areas for many of Britain's rarest bird species.

Without realising, I passed by another ancient barrow mound, this one called Wheeldale Howe, similar in size to Shunner Howe. Maybe the dead there watched me pass, wondering whether I belonged in their world or the mortal one. It would have been easy to be mistaken; I was becoming cadaver-grey, and staggering as if I were taking my final steps.

Once again I was using a lot of effort for very little movement. Trips and falls were common. I got out my compass to check that I was running ('running' in the loosest sense of the word) in the right direction. I thought I had drifted too far south, so decided to swing a bit more north to make sure I found the tiny track.

It seemed an age since we had climbed out of the car in the downpour at Osmotherley. Since then I'd nearly succumbed to hypothermia, got completely soaked and wind-blown, could have run round in circles in zero visibility in a maelstrom, fallen off crags, drowned in peat bog, I'd suffered repeated painful cramps, felt sick, and now I was being beaten up by deep, spiky and abrasive heather. And in the planning of the event all I was worried about was sunburn!

It was beginning to dawn on me that this run was possibly a stupid idea. Clearly I'm not that bright. Most people would have realised it was a stupid idea long before now.• I had endured several hours of physical abuse and the end was still not in sight. What was in sight, however, was another sizeable hill to go over once - if - I cleared the next checkpoint.

I managed to find the path just lurking under the brow of Wheeldale Beck, and immediately had a nasty fall, whacking my right knee. But I wasn't bothered about that as it didn't hurt anywhere near as much as the excruciatingly unyielding cramp in my left thigh and hip. I lay in the heather for a few minutes trying to unlock the knotted, contorted muscles, while screaming a multitude of swear words. Fortunately there was no one around to be offended by my profanity. Nearest to me was the Blue Man, a few hundred yards back, and I'm guessing he could neither hear, nor care.

Sunburn? How about exhaustion and collapse on a desolate moor?

The spasm subsided, I hauled myself to my feet, and headed eastwards once again on a trail that snaked and wound through heather and bracken before pointing itself at Wheeldale Road, where I hoped Andy would be waiting. I didn't know for sure because reception on the replacement radio was rubbish. No Norman Collier or Stephen Hawking, just the sound of bacon sizzling in a hot pan. Bacon! Mmmmmmm, what would I have given for a bacon sandwich? And a cup of tea!

I reached the checkpoint with no further mishaps. Andy *was* there, and Justin too, who I described as dirty and tired. In hindsight this was probably an appalling case of the pot calling the kettle black.

The nauseous feeling was intensifying. I drank some water and thanked them both before setting off almost immediately down to Wheeldale Beck, a sizeable stream that had to be crossed. Controlling my increasingly disobedient legs on descents was becoming troublesome, and I bounced erratically down the steep valley sides to the stream.

I could smell the wet bracken as it brushed against me, a smell that reminded me that it *was* still summer. My shoes gave out the occasional squeak as they slipped ever so slightly on the wet carpet of grass beneath. It was obvious from some distance away that the beck was in flood. It looked like a gushing torrent some twenty feet wide. Four walkers were standing on the far bank, surveying the river, looking for a possible place to cross. They gave up and turned back the way they had come. This didn't fill me with hope.

On my final few paces of the descent-cum-crashland to the stream I almost stepped on an adder that was resting on a streamside stone. The snake must have come out from its hiding hole to try and warm up in the faint sunshine that was still sulking instead of accepting its responsibilities consistent with the month of July. Fortunately for the both of us I missed stepping on it, and it didn't feel the need to bite me.

I planned not to stop to think about the river crossing. I hurriedly checked for a good way over, and could see what looked like stepping-stones, but they were submerged beneath two feet of gushing water. Rushing headlong at a swollen beck after having run 30 miles through swamps may not be sensible, but sense handed in its notice when we got up that morning. In its absence bravado once again grabbed the controls and ploughed me into the beck, aiming for the stepping-stones. Bravado had a bad aim.

Right foot slid off to the side, left foot tried to compensate but was pushed away by the force of the torrent, and I went head first in a flurry of waving arms and spraying water. Great! Add snakebite and drowning to that *risk list* that initially started and finished with sunburn.

Somehow my left arm connected with one of the stepping-stones, I was able to keep most of my upper body above the water, and maintaining forward momentum I eventually dragged myself out the other side. The four walkers had been watching. Now totally convinced that crossing the beck was not a good idea they turned their backs on it for good and began walking away in earnest. I casually tried jogging up the hill towards Hunt House Crag, trying to give them the impression that I always went through streams like that, and that nothing significant had happened so far today.

After the climb up to the Crag the gradient lessened towards Simon Howe Rigg, on top of which is apparently another tumulus of standing stones, but I didn't see it. The path passed Simon Howe on the left, then headed due east over a flat kilometre, with the small rise of Crag Stone Rigg just to the right before another kilometre of straight, fast downhill which, though awkward and painful, was nevertheless a joy to descend.

I had viewed this trail from the main A169 road that we had travelled along towards Robin Hood's Bay. It looked a great run, partly smooth, partly rocky, 'yee-haa-ing' straight down the hillside. And it was! The descent culminated in the crossing of the track of the North York Moors Railway line, which at 18 miles in length is the second longest heritage railway line in the UK.

Running between Grosmont and Pickering, the line is mainly operated and staffed by volunteers who drive the beautiful steam engines mostly as a hugely popular and well-used tourist attraction. The North Yorkshire Moors Railway line was planned by George Stevenson (probably the most famous son of Chesterfield, where I currently live) in 1831, and opened in 1836 to form trade routes inland from the port of Whitby. It was an engineering breakthrough of its time, involving amongst other things cutting one of the first railway tunnels in the world (120 yards through rock at Grosmont), crossing a marshy bog on a base of timber and sheep fleeces, and constructing a steep rope incline system.

The line is unbelievably picturesque, and the stations renovated in period style. It has been used in numerous television programs and major cinematic movies, most notably Goathland station featured as Hogsmeade Station in the *Harry Potter* films.

Not wanting to add 'hit by train' to my ever-growing list of potential cause of death, I stopped and carefully looked both ways before setting foot on the track. No smoke or steam in sight, no sound of a whistle, no

Hogwarts Express, so I crossed, joined a wide path and I was almost at checkpoint six at Eller Beck Bridge, where my wife was waiting.

Dragging myself wearily up the bank to the road, I could see our car in a lay-by, with the two Andreas standing next to it. There was no sign of the crew car. A brief gap in the traffic careering up the A169 allowed my crossing, and I jogged over to be told that I was lucky they were still there. They had been waiting quite a while and were about to leave, thinking I had already passed through. Andy and Justin were at an alternative checkpoint tending to Mal.

Andrea tried to keep a straight face when she saw me, but failed to disguise that look someone has when they smell something decaying. I knew I had turned into a fetid, stinking, hobbling filthy monster. I had embarked on the journey of the dead, and was beginning to smell like death.

She even told me that I looked awful, and that she couldn't imagine how I was managing to keep moving. The other Andrea agreed. This is the kind of honesty that doesn't usually make for a good support-team motivational pep talk. The usual crew had perfected the positive ("You look great, you're doing great, you'll easily make it to the finish") big, fat, barefaced lies that would leave Pinocchio with a four-foot proboscis, but would actually make one believe that they would actually, against all odds, get to the finish. Even if clearly they couldn't. A positive mental attitude is everything.

I was becoming increasingly dehydrated, and energy levels were getting very low. I asked the ladies what supplies they had.

"Supplies?" came the surprised reply.

"Yes, cake, biscuits, drink, anything."

"We've not got anything."

"Only the last bit of water in this bottle," added the other Andrea, holding out a mostly empty plastic bottle that once contained clear, refreshing, thirst quenching, cooling, life-giving, delightful, glorious water; the last few drops of which glistened temptingly and drummed inside the plastic bottle as she shook it to show me. That was like throwing crumbs of bread into the wind in front of a starving man.

"Nothing then!" I must have looked disappointed.

"Sorry, no. Nothing."

But what they *did* have was my MP3 music player in the glove compartment of the car. That would have to do as some form of pain relief or distraction to try and get me the last few miles to civilisation. I clipped the device onto the chest strap of my pack, next to the radio (that was actually little more than a heavy and cumbersome ornament), and popped the earphones into my sweaty, mud-filled lobes. I thanked the ladies for their assistance (only partly sarcastically as they didn't *have* to be there to support me), and went to kiss Andrea. She took a step back and said I'd get one once I had been cleaned up. I think she really meant *decontaminated*. Charming! No food, no drink, not even a kiss from my wife, so I set off through the gate and along the path eastwards up Eller Beck. The MP3 player shuffled songs randomly and fed my ears with a soundtrack to my suffering.

After initially curving to the right the small trail took a left, and I had to jump the main stream that gushed thousands of gallons of chocolate-brown water, cutting a deep gash through the reeds and peat. A feeble path followed a tiny tributary, Little Eller Beck, up towards Lilla Howe.

The suffering increased. I had hauled myself further than 30 miles, but it wasn't the distance alone that was draining every ounce of effort from my battered body. Although about to go further than I had ever done before in a single run I truly believed 43 miles was within my capabilities. I had also ploughed my way through sections of sticky, heavy mud on previous runs. But the distance and conditions combined were grinding me into the dirt.

Every time I looked at the map the trails moved as if I was looking at a bowl of spaghetti that the waiter was swirling round. A combination of leg cramps, foot blisters and a very narrow, gulley-like and winding path made keeping balance challenging. Just like Jackson's Path, water gushed along making this more like a river than a trail.

I was limping and hunched, filthy and smelly, wobbling and hobbling, stumbling and bouncing my way along in a spray of splashing water and a flurry of waving arms and splaying, uncontrollable legs. The MP3 player injected a rock song into my ears that I mostly recognised but didn't quite know the lyrics to. Trying to sing along I mumbled groaning noises and half-uttered, mispronounced words. It suddenly dawned on me that I must have appeared a bizarre sight, and I laughed aloud as I realised what I reminded myself of - *Frankenstein's monster*, groaning and lurching painfully forward in a bid to escape the angry mob that was trying to drive him out of town.

Laughing at my pathetic state, I peered behind me. Thankfully there was nobody. No belligerent crowd of peasants and villagers armed with pitchforks and burning sticks, intent on seeing me off. I looked forwards again, then down at the trail to check my footing, and almost stepped on a man's face.

***

Death for the King

The picture of a late-middle-aged man stared up at me as it drifted meanderingly down the path-cum-stream. His happy-looking eyes peered from behind black-rimmed spectacles, and he seemed delighted to be out on the moors, even while printed out on A4 paper. Underneath the face was printed a name, which escapes me now, but it was a good solid name, the kind of name that belongs to someone born to be wild; a hill walker, an adventurer, a climber. A dead man!

Underneath the name were three boldly printed words: 'Rest in Peace'. And then, printed on the next line, the knockout punch, "Missed by all your walking mates". I stopped and stood, wobbling slightly, and staring at the face as it sailed dreamily past on a trip of its own. He smiled at me, then the paper spun round in the current and he peered over to the west.

The hairs on the back of my neck tingled. Was he here, the man with the solid name? Was he on the moor, watching, resting, taking time out from his own arduous last journey to paradise. I could feel something profound, something deep and emotional, happy and sad, painful but numb. He clearly loved this place enough for his walking mates to bring him here, to be here forever.

What should I do? Should I lift him out of the stream and put him in the heather. No! I let him go. The solid name was smiling and happy, drifting through the moors wherever they took him; he was in the water, in the peat, in the heather. He *was* the moor, and he was happy.

I was fatigued and emotional, and couldn't spend my eternity standing here, and in my exhausted state found I was deeply affected by the tribute to the man with the solid name. Tears welled up uncontrollably, but I didn't know why. Perhaps it was being touched by death while in the middle of my epic journey, particularly the death of a man who loved being where I loved being, although I never knew him. Perhaps it was somehow a realisation that life always hangs by a thread, and that thread had been dangled all too close to home the last few months; and while alive we must live, breath the fresh air, feel the earth, and be part of nature.

Emotions wrestled within me. I felt wonderful and wretched, elated and devastated, angry yet serenely calm. I felt alive! I was exhausted but energised. I had to get moving again, and started splashing my way up the hill, sniffing, almost sobbing. The previous song on the MP3 player finished, and *DJ Fate* spun the next one. The lyrics to Green Day's 'Boulevard of Broken Dreams' pierced my conscience, poured my cocktail of contrasting emotions into a blender, switched it to 'fast whisk', and I became a gibbering, hobbling mess:

> *I walk a lonely road, the only one that I have ever known*
> *Don't know where it goes but it's only me and I walk alone.*

I stumbled clumsily along, listening intently to Green Day, who had a message that appeared to be aimed directly at me,

> *Check my vital signs, I know I'm still alive and I walk alone...*

The path became increasingly narrow and winding, and I started to look for a better route. A hundred yards to my right was a gravel track, heading in the right direction, on the edge of Ministry of Defence land. Surely that was a better option, and I didn't think I'd get into trouble as long as I didn't stray to the other side of the track and past the signs reading: 'MOD LAND. KEEP OUT'.

I abandoned the stream and started beating a way through the heather. The heather started beating back. Once again it threw me sideways, twisted my joints and sapped my energy. Those hundred yards must have taken five minutes, but once on the track I was moving quickly again. The hobbling-shuffle became a slow jog as I was able at last to find a rhythm and get my legs moving as the joints intended.

Then the jog sped up slightly, and clean, cool air flowed across my face, wiping away my sniffles like a mother's tissue. It was only moments before I crossed a wide path that ran perpendicular to the main track, and found myself at the brow of the hill, which was adorned with the dramatic stone cross at *Lilla Howe*.

The cross stands above a barrow that has been found to contain Viking and Saxon grave artefacts. Lilla Cross, the oldest and grandest Christian monument on the North York Moors, once formed the boundaries of four medieval parishes, and the edge of the estate belonging to Whitby Abbey in the eleventh century. The cross is named after a seventh century Saxon nobleman who was killed saving the life of the king. Lilla was the chief minister to King Edwin of Northumbria. In 625 AD he threw himself between Edwin and an assassin, suffering fatal wounds as a result.

A middle aged couple sat beneath the cross, drinking tea from a flask. Those cups of tea looked magnificent; steaming slightly, not too much milk, probably the perfect temperature to gulp down to refresh a Sahara thirst. And maybe they contained a spoonful of sugar or two. And what else was in their rucksack? Biscuits? Cake? Maybe a chocolate éclair stuffed so full with whipped cream that it oozed out of each end and mixed with the soft chocolate that had been liberally poured over the top. Stop it!!

Desperate times call for desperate measures, but I couldn't stoop so low as to mug a couple of walkers for their mid-afternoon picnic. Besides, had I made a lunge for their victuals, the ghost of Lilla may well have arisen and leapt between us. I didn't have the energy to repel a long-dead ancient spirit, never mind a couple of angry ramblers. I forced a smile and nodded politely in reply to their cheery "Hello", and ran on, trying to ignore the demons that screamed "Steal the tea, steal the cake".

From the brow I could see a long downhill section stretching for over two miles in front of me. This would help enormously, the pace would be good and the end would be creeping ever nearer. As I set off trotting I allowed my eyes to rise up to the far horizon, and what was that I could see almost straight in front? A very flat, grey thing that looked a lot like....yes it was... it was the sea! And a bit to the right on that hill top not a million miles away...could it be?...it looks like...wait...yes it is. It's the mast, the mast on the hill just above the hotel at Ravenscar.

I tried to focus to see it clearly, and could see it reasonably clearly whenever both my eyeballs stopped rolling and pointed in the same direction. It was definitely a thin sticking up thing, pointing out from the top of a hill just this side of the sea. What else could it be? I was nearly there.

The last few metres of the long and tiring descent proved tough as the track divided and plummeted into a steep, slippery, muddy gulley. My thigh muscles screamed as I fought to control speed and direction and prevent a head first dive into the mud. Thankfully a wooden bridge provided easy crossing of this stream and I didn't have to risk drowning again.

The hill up the other side of the beck was ridiculously steep with some mud and loose stones that made the surface like running on a treadmill – too much effort for too little movement. I found it almost impossible to climb out from the river. There had evidently been far too much gravity built into this part of the hill. If I could have called him back on the radio I would have asked Stephen Hawking to investigate Jugger Howe Beck. It defied the known laws of physics. I'd swear there was a black hole nearby pulling everything back towards it.

I leaned forward and stretched out my hands to ascend on all fours. My legs pushed reluctantly, my feet slid backwards, my stomach hit the ground and I lay prostrate on the 45 degree slope. Inside, my abused lower limbs hurled obscenities and decided to go on an unscheduled and indefinite tea break. A walkout by a significant body part was something I really didn't need right then.

My brain was desperately calling my legs to get them to work, but there was no reply. The legs had gone on strike and had their answer-phone switched on:

"Hello, this is the legs. We're sorry but we can't take your call right now as we've been viciously abused and left for dead on a Yorkshire moor. Please leave a message and we'll get back to you when we can. Alternatively dial 1 if you wish to collapse, or dial 2 to send for mountain rescue services."

"Legs, this is brain. Pick up and talk to me."

No reply! Brain tried again.

"Legs, I know you're there. Pick up."

"No. Go away."

I lay there a bit longer whilst brain tried a different approach.

"Listen, legs. You've done really well. There's not far to go now. Just up this next hill is the last checkpoint. Then it's only three miles to the finish. When you get there you can have tea and cakes."

Silence from legs.

"And a good sit down!" added brain, for good measure.

There was a general grumbling from the lower limbs as they consulted each other. Consensus was reached. Legs decided it would be better to battle on further for the promise of cake than to spend a cold and wet night dangling on a steep hillside. I raised my head and looked up my Everest which, although only short, appeared in my mind to extend far towards the chinks of blue that gazed teasingly down through the thinning cloud cover.

I lifted myself once again, on to all fours at first, and slowly started an infant-like crawl up the slippery slope. Progress was slow but sure, and occasional scrapings of soil from the soles of my shoes shot back to the stream. All the time my ears, which were oblivious to any suffering, continued their own relaxing afternoon. I'd swear a higher presence was controlling the playlist on my MP3 player, as Gary Barlow offered some useful advice:

Just have a little patience.

Gary told my ears that he was feeling my frustration, and any minute all the pain would stop. But my ears continued to take it easy and neglected to convey the ridiculously optimistic message to the rest of my body.

The gradient eased, and over the distance of a few struggled steps I recreated the evolution of man – slowly morphing from four-legged ape, through knuckle dragging half-human, to Homo Sapiens. I was upright again, and planned to stay that way.

The path became a track wide enough to drive a car down, and I could see from the map that the last checkpoint before the finish was only a few hundred yards away. This short distance passed without incident, and I passed the barrow of Jugger Howe without even noticing.

The sky was bluer, the air warming, and the next song to play was mood lightening. Take That's 'Beautiful World' warmed my soul and sent me a message of hope:

The sun will shine, and we will see
There's nothing standing in our way.

But there was. Justin was standing in my way as I rounded the bend into the car park on the side of the A171. He called to Andy and the Andrea's, informing them of my imminent arrival.

The ladies climbed out of the car and greeted me with mixed expressions. There seemed to be raised eyebrows of surprise that I was still moving, curled noses of disgust at the smell, and tight-lipped grimaces of concern as to how ill I looked. Not the expressions you see on the front cover of *Vogue*. More like *Horse and Hound*!

They both told me how terrible I looked. I thanked them for their honesty.

Justin looked at me like he was trying to remember his cardio-pulmonary-resuscitation training. Andy just shouted "Weyyyyheyyyyy".

Offers of food were refused, as I was too nauseus. A few sips of water were all I could manage before I started off for the final section. There were only three miles to go. I wasn't going to let it slip away now.

With head high I aimed resolutely to cross the road, before being held upright by Andrea. My gyroscopes had gone, and with them went much of the control over my direction. I was looking east, leaning north, drifting slightly southwards, and wobbling around all points of the compass in a random manner. Like a boy scout helping an old lady across the road, my wife assisted me to the other side of the A171.

Once safely across and having avoided becoming road kill I thanked her, told her I loved her, said I'd see her at the hotel in half an hour, and disappeared over the embankment and onto the final moor.

***

I wondered if this was what chemotherapy felt like. Was this what Andrea had been suffering for several days at a time? I was aching from everywhere I could think of, my head was pounding, I was dizzy and retching but with nothing coming up. To move was to hurt. Death would have felt like blessed relief. Jeez, that must have been some ordeal for Andrea. And she had suffered six rounds of this, poisoned every three weeks for more than four months. To reach the same wretched state I'd had to run for eight hours straight, through the hardest, muddiest, stickiest conditions I had ever encountered, whilst becoming increasingly dehydrated.

How much courage must it have taken to allow the needle to be pushed into her arm time and time again, to have the lines connected, the syringes joined up and the drugs slowly but determinedly injected and oozed into every living cell?

Maybe I did feel the same - it was how I imagined it having seen her suffering – maybe I didn't, but I was putting myself through this for my own bizarre pleasure. Andrea had no choice, no alternative, and definitely no pleasure. She didn't do what she did just for herself, she also did it for me, for Hannah and William, for our parents and friends and everyone else who wanted and needed her with us.

I wanted her with me now, but she wasn't here on this grassy track that slowly made its way in a straight line up an easy hill towards the mast. But she wasn't far away, just over this next lump of land that balanced on the edge of the sea, holding onto the moors by its fingertips.

The little hill looked like it might imminently lose its grip on its bigger brothers and sisters and fall into the sea, taking Raven Hall Hotel and a few hundred acres of land with it. Unknowingly I had been bent double close to the five barrows of Stony Marl Howes. Thankfully I wasn't sick disrespectfully close to the dead, but I feared I might be.

I stood upright and jogged onwards again; hoping the urges to vomit had finished. DJ Irony pumped my ears full of 'Speed of Sound' by Coldplay. That's a laugh! I was struggling with *speed of snail*. A few hundred yards and it would be all over.

I crested the hill, ran past the mast (giving it barely a glance), and also ran past the finishing stone of the Lyke Wake walk without ever seeing it, in much the same way that we had missed the stone at the start. Next came a short track to the left, I pushed through some bracken by a wall and climbed a stone stile. Falling away in front of me was the grassy field I had seen from the hotel room the day before, and beyond that I could see the hotel itself, tucked beyond its tree-lined driveway.

With a yelp of delight I took off the brakes and went into fast-footed free-fall down the field. This was steeper than I anticipated, and required a great amount of effort to maintain balance and a safe speed. My legs screamed at me once again as I forced them to persist, pounding like pistons to stop me at the bottom. The limbs moaned to each other that this wasn't part of the deal we'd made at Jugger Howe Beck, and wanted to know where the cake and a good sit-down was.

After a right turn and a short jog up a narrow lane I came to the tarmac road that led to the hotel. Looking down I could see it, a mere quarter of a mile away, and there by the gates was Andrea, looking anxiously back up the road towards me.

All pain evaporated. Running became simple and natural. My body, accepting the end was imminent, let go all resistance. My movements were smooth, and flowed as easily as the tears that now flowed from my salty, stinging eyes. Covered in filth, sweat and bits of moorland debris, and bursting with love and pride, I was about to finish. The 'higher being' spun one last song through my MP3: the encore, the finale to the soundtrack of a stupendous ultra-marathon - 'Crazy', by Seal. Perfect!

> *But we're never gonna survive*
> *Unless we get a little crazy.*

***

Why?

It's a question that is raised almost every time the exploits of an ultra-distance run are described. (Close behind it is the question, how?) Why do you do it, why put yourself through it? The reasons are complex, difficult to explain, and I can't say that I understand them.

There's certainly a large element of testing yourself, accepting a challenge, trying to find your limits; it's comparable to George Leigh Mallory's attitude to Everest - "because it's there".

Completing a difficult challenge brings a huge amount of satisfaction, and there is pleasure in the planning, training, and anticipation, especially if teamwork and camaraderie are involved. Super-long distance running requires a slow, steady pace, so when ultra-runners run together they often chat, help each other out and exchange stories. We are a sociable bunch.

But we're still barely scratching the surface. The 'why' cuts far deeper.

The prolonged physical exertion causes physiological and biochemical changes within the body. There is an increase in levels of neurotransmitters, such as serotonin (a 'happy' chemical), and dopamine, which plays a role in addiction. Levels of natural opiates - endorphins (morphine made by the body) - are raised, which has a euphoric effect. Recent studies on runners have also highlighted higher levels of a chemical called phenylethylamine, which boosts mood as quickly as amphetamines but without the side effects. These sensations can be felt by running shorter distances than ultra-marathons, but ultra-runners get whacked with a rock-and-roll overdose.

These natural 'drugs' don't eliminate the pain, but help make it an acceptable part of the process. Their increased presence means a runner may experience periods of ecstasy, joy, clarity in thinking and profound calmness. Over the course of a long run these effects can be cyclic, which would explain my own ultra-running emotional volatility. Pain and pleasure ride hand in hand on the roller-coaster ride within mind and body. Scream if you want to go faster.

As well as the emotional, there are philosophical aspects to long solo running. It is escapism, a way to lose yourself, and find yourself. Often it hurts, but, *damn*, it feels good.

An ultra distance run is like setting off into an uncharted cave. It may be dark, difficult and painful. But then you find yourself in a fantastic cavern with sights that are like nothing you have seen before, uplifting, indescribably beautiful rock formations, magnificent stalactites, stalagmites, crystals and gems. But then you slide back into another tunnel, maybe heading for the next, even better, cavern. If you gave up when it was dark and painful you would never reach the undiscovered beauty.

To quote a phrase I read from the excellent getultrarunning.eu website: "To those who know, no explanation is necessary. To those who do not know, no explanation will suffice."

***

Everyone was by the hotel gates as, after 43 miles of wondrous torture, I pulled to a stop and grabbed Andrea for a long and emotional hug. I was done, in all senses of the word. Mal's muddied bike was leaning against a signpost where he had abandoned it after his own long and arduous journey. The heavy conditions and lack of a straight bike-friendly route across the moors had slowed him significantly, and he had eventually beaten me to the finish by just a couple of minutes. Thankfully, his collarbone stayed intact and didn't cause him any suffering.

Justin and Andy snapped away with their cameras. We celebrated the ordeal with a rash of hugs and general backslapping, and then strolled into the hotel car park where I finally enjoyed a rest.

After eight hours and 22 minutes of running, walking, crawling, slipping, sliding, stumbling, falling and generally dragging myself through moorland bogs I dropped my CamelBak to the gravelly floor and lay on the ground. Andy produced a hip flask containing my favourite single malt whisky, and I took a long, hard drink before staring up at the sky, smiling like a crazed lunatic.

As I lay prostrate the last few wispy clouds that remained from the earlier maelstrom parted, and a big, bright, orange July sun held back no longer and radiated its summer fierceness onto us. Now where did I put that sun cream?

The two Andreas went through the impressive entrance and into the hotel to get washed and changed for dinner. Mal ferreted around in Andy's car boot, looking for the water container so he could wash most of the mud off his bike before storing it in the back of his car. After a few more satisfying gulps from the hip flask I endeavoured to raise myself from the floor, in a manner very reminiscent of the early scene in the film *Bambi*, where the young deer tries to walk for the first time. Justin and Andy played the parts of Thumper and Flower, giggling childishly as I wobbled and tottered erratically towards them, threatening to fall with legs splayed at any moment.

I pulled off most of my wet, muddy, cold clothes and stuffed them into a plastic bag to try and contain the fusty stench emanating from every thread. Shoes and socks were removed to reveal a pair of wrinkled feet that were coated in brown, smelly slime. After eight hours immersed in a solution of muddy, sweaty water they didn't look good.

Shivering and covered in goose bumps I threw on an old sweater and a pair of baggy jogging trousers – just enough to make myself sufficiently decent not to be evicted from the hotel lobby. Then, with more *Bambi-on-ice* I set off in the rough direction of the hotel. Fortunately I'd left the hip flask in the car. Had I still been waving it around as I staggered through the doors dressed like a tramp, face covered in mud, sweat and tears, and smelling of peat bog and whisky I wouldn't have made it over the threshold before security sent me packing back towards Osmotherley.

The stairs up to the first floor provided less of a challenge than they had after the coast-to-coast. Andrea let me into our room, and I was greeted with a kiss and the watery sound of a steaming hot bath being run. To add heavenly bliss, the kettle had just boiled and a cup of tea was slowly wafting its fragrant delights while sitting on a saucer, guarded by two biscuits. I hoped the dead of ancient Yorkshire had as good a welcome after their journey.

Slowly lowering myself into the bath was sheer and utter pleasure, and would have been even better had the bath been large enough to comfortably accommodate my six-foot frame. Alas, I was unable to submerge myself and leave only my nostrils above the surface to continue breathing. I would happily have lain in that bath forever, had it been a comfortable size.

Instead I had either to bend my knees and have them stick out of the water, or sit with legs straight and be unable to hot-soak my torso. I apologised to the legs once again, and went for the knees-up soak, although this made sipping the tea much harder. (The biscuits had already gone – wolfed down in seconds.)

Comfort at last; warmth, safety, a chance to doze. But I was foolish to let my guard down. I started to wash, and leaned forward to apply soap to my left leg. With my new level of muscular stiffness there was not enough room in the bath to get into the position I needed to reach my feet. So I stretched further. Sudden and violent cramps made me jerk and twist round, and I found myself submerged face-down in the tight space, head underwater, terrified and unable to breathe.

A few seconds of petrified thrashing followed, like bagged and struggling kittens thrown into the canal, before I righted myself and gasped, panicking for air. Waves shot round the tub like an ocean storm and gushed over the sides, flooding the floor. I'd just had another close escape. Dangers lurk everywhere with this ultra-running malarkey. Hypothermia, falls off cliffs, sinking in bogs, swollen rivers, snakes, *AND* drowning in the bath afterwards. How I wished I'd just got sunburned.

***

The manner in which I comfortably ambled downstairs to breakfast the next morning asked more questions than it answered. I felt only slightly sore, mostly in my thighs and calves, otherwise great. The Lyke Wake had been long and tough. I had carved a 43-mile furrow across, up and down the boggy, sticky, energy-sapping, and body-beating North York Moors, and although having suffered, I still had plenty of life and movement to bounce the final half-mile once my brain took the brakes off.

Everyone else marvelled at my surprising mobility too.

"Aren't you stiff?"

"How can you still walk?"

"Are you hungry?"

I *was* hungry, very hungry, and set to work piling in huge quantities of food.

I was beginning to learn that there is no finish line with ultra-distance running. The questions never go away: How far could I go with better training, with better nutrition, hydration, and preparation? What are *my* limits of endurance? What would it feel like to run 50 miles, 100 miles? Curiosity threatens to kill ultra-running cats.

If the desire for discovery and a constant challenge was part of the 'why' of ultra-running then I couldn't stop now. How long would it take before the aches and pains of yesterday's run were forgotten, and the question of 'what next' reared its inevitable head? These were dangerous thoughts.

But first I had to register my crossing with the Lyke Wake Club, and stake my claim to being a Dirger.

***

*Standing between Mal and Justin at the start of the Lyke Wake attempt.
The middle of summer!!*

With Justin at checkpoint 4.

Stumbling with a painful hip onto Wheeldale road.

Exhausted at the finish, with Mal.

The team at Ravenscar.

Grit

The rest of the summer of 2007 was mostly given over to rebuilding. Andrea had to rebuild a body ravaged by cancer treatment. As well as the drugs and radiation, the disease had forced her into a prolonged period of inactivity. Her initial weight loss that was caused by sickness had rebounded into steroid and stagnation-induced weight gain.

A regime of healthy eating and gradually increasing activity levels began to reverse the malaise. The radiation burns had almost completely healed two weeks after the final fraction of radiotherapy. Her hair was starting to return, but would remain too short to be styled for several months. Although it would take a long time she was determined to return to her previous level of fitness. It was the middle of August before she had recovered sufficient energy to return to work.

There was no more treatment to have. From now on it would be a case of regular follow up appointments with Dr Purohit, and yearly mammograms (X-ray of the breast) to ensure no new lumps were appearing. Initially she was to see the oncologist every three months.

For me, the rebuilding involved taking time off from running to let muscles, joints and tendons recover and strengthen. Running shoes were abandoned in the garage (far too stinking to be inside the house) for a week after the Lyke Wake, and I only jogged 30 miles in total in the following month.

We tried to take it easy, relax, and have fun as a family, fun that the cancer had done its evil best to steal from us since Andrea's diagnosis. There were only two races in my calendar before the much anticipated trip to New York, and these were both in early September. The first was the 'Spire 10', a local ten-mile road race that has a hilly, circular loop; the course starts with a 700ft climb towards the edge of the Peak District.

The second was the Chatsworth Challenge.

Continuing our theme of having a fun summer, Mal, Andrea and Vin came to stay with us for a barbecue party the day before the Spire 10. The race was my first since the Worksop half marathon, almost a year before. I wondered whether the recent moorland slog had stripped me of any speed. It hadn't. I managed a personal best time for the course: 1 hour 8 minutes. But I was nowhere near Vin. He was charging near the front of the race, finishing in eighth place in a time of 1 hour and thirty seconds. Those thirty seconds would have bothered me, but Vin seemed cool with them.

The Chatsworth Challenge was the following weekend, and this was a completely different beast: longer, tougher, and off-road, some of it very steep and rocky. At twenty-five miles in length this wasn't technically an ultra-marathon, but the difficulty of the terrain made it harder than some flat ultra-distance events.

The route passes through the White and Dark areas of the Peak District, and the event itself is tackled by both runners and challenge walkers.

I wasn't worried about the distance but it was a tough course. I was pleased that drinks and biscuits would be provided at the seven checkpoints *en-route*, and better still, a plate of pie and peas would be served at the finish.

Two years previously I had run the course twice: once to check it out, and the other time with Vin in the official race. Vin had won, I had finished fifth after going out too hard and fading as the event progressed. This time I didn't have Vin to pull me too quickly up the first hill, and I was committed to more sensible tactics in the belief that if I ran well I could once again be placed in the top five.

***

The brightness of the morning sun threatened to exceed the expectations of September as I drove the six miles to Baslow, on the outskirts of Chatsworth Park. The time was 7.30 in the morning, and the remaining few stubborn clouds showed signs of dispersing rather than amassing. Yet the chill in the air told that summer was steadily burning out.

The huge golden gates at the north end of the Park loomed gloriously large, and I was ushered through and directed to leave my car on the grass beside the lane that led to the magnificent Chatsworth House. The House, which is the seat of the Duke of Devonshire, stands on the east bank of the river Derwent, and is backed by dramatic hills cloaked in mature woodland that extends upwards to heather moorland. In front stretch sizeable parkland and gardens that are hugely popular with tourists.

Many other competitors milled around the parking field, some tying up walking boots, others checking rucksacks, and some runners were trotting around to get warm. A few ambled in the direction of Baslow village hall, from where the event would start.

The morning chill presented the dilemma of what to wear. I gambled on the day getting warmer, and decided to run light. Leggings were removed to reveal a pair of shorts, and ankle socks poking out of the top of my trail shoes. On my top half I wore a tight, white t-shirt made from technical wicking fibres that were designed to keep me dry from my own sweat. Over that I pulled on a lightweight windproof jacket just to stop me shivering before setting off. My CamelBak rucksack was relegated to the car boot. Instead I took a small bumbag that would accommodate my jacket. It also held an emergency gel sachet in case I required urgent calories late in the race.

The village hall was far too small to accommodate all 300 entrants; walkers and runners spilled out into the car park, several accompanied by well behaved dogs that all looked eager. After squeezing into the hall and registering, I squeezed back outside and stretched in a quiet corner of the car park. I had been given a card that was to be stamped at every checkpoint to prove I had run the correct course. This was stuffed into the smaller pocket of my bumbag. The start was moments away.

At 8.30 we were called forward to the village green, a mixed rabble of walkers, relaxed looking runners, and excitable dogs. The atmosphere was far less serious than the road racing business. The button on the pelican crossing was pressed to stop the traffic flowing along the main road through the village, and we were politely invited to set off. It was all very courteous, very well-mannered, and there were no elbows out to get to the front. But that didn't mean the runners weren't taking it seriously.

The polite mass stretched into a mobile, linear gathering as everyone headed up the first long and steep climb. I was comfortably pottering along on the shoulders of the two leaders as the road swung right, turned into a rocky track and attacked the hill head on. The ascent was over a mile in length, and I knew I had to take it easy. Recklessness was reined-in as firstly I let the two leaders go, and then allowed three others to pass me as I slowed to a fast walk. There were 25 miles and 4,000 feet of climbing and descending before the finish back in Baslow. The race wouldn't be won by a sprint to the first summit.

At the top of Baslow Edge I was still in sixth place and feeling fresh. The route headed northwards to the gritstone crags of Curbar Edge. Overhead the last remnants of the morning cloud had dissolved away and the day was becoming glorious. The views into the White Peak to the west were stunning, but I didn't have time to enjoy them.

After the big climb came a gradual uphill to the high point of the Edge. Dramatic gritstone cliffs plummeted down to the left. I continued to hold back, waiting for my time to run hard. I could see four runners stretched between 100 and 300 yards ahead. The leader was out of sight. But I was happy. I had no expectations to win, I just hoped to run well and be somewhere around the top five.

Rocky cliffs made from 'millstone grit' line many miles of the east side of the Peak District. The 'grits' are sandstone deposits laid down 300 million years ago by a huge river that flowed from mountains in the north-eastern part of Britain, as it was then. Differing layers of rock have eroded at differing rates over the millennia, leaving the tough gritstone edges that stand ominous guard high over the valleys.

"What are they doing?" I thought as I rapidly caught up with the four who were standing, looking down the first rocky drop-off. Had someone taken a bad fall? Then I realised that they were simply assessing the best way down. This *was* a tricky section, but only very short, and there were no reasons to stop to examine it. At that point I knew I could win a huge psychological battle.

I never cast the four a glance as I launched myself past them and over the edge, bounding confidently and swiftly from rock to rock with the agility of a mountain goat, continuing until the track evened out again and I was able to switch back to even-tempo running. Behind I could hear grunts and groans, huffing and puffing as the others crashed awkwardly down before running hard to try and catch me. I had just passed four runners who were three hundred yards ahead simply by using confidence and good technique.

Just around the next corner was the start of the toughest, steepest, most dangerous downhill on the course. This was my chance to have some fun. At least one runner was on my shoulder as I turned off the main path and down through some rocks under Froggatt Edge.

Almost immediately the trail switched back to the left, and there, on the corner, was the leader. He was gingerly picking his way slowly down the trail. This wasn't the time to run gingerly. I leapt over a cluster of boulders that lurked in wait to snap unwary ankles, and ducked under a low tree branch, pulling on the tree trunk with my left arm to steer me into the centre of the trail that cut through ancient woodland. Then my brain loaded the 'downhill specialist' software, and went into freefall along the steep, winding path that was beset with traps of all kinds: boulders, loose stones, tree roots, low branches, stream beds, moss and mud.

There were also a few man-made obstacles. Evenly formed sections of gritstone, devoid of lines of weakness, were put to use by stonemasons who carved them into round stones that were used to grind wheat and barley in the local mills – hence the name 'millstone grit'. Some half-chiselled millstones, broken during manufacture many years ago, lay abandoned near the path, as they do in many locations throughout the area.

Panting and grinning, I burst across the road at the bottom of the hill, startling the two marshals in the process, and then zipped down the next field to the lane that led to the river. I had wreaked mayhem on the race behind; there was nobody close. But the next section involved another long uphill. Could I hold on without pushing too hard? There were still over 20 miles to go, after all.

Half way up the hill the path crossed a lane. There stood a drinks station. I was offered water, but declined. I could see the second placed runner about two minutes behind. Had I really made that much time on one small descent? Quickly I formulated a plan. If I could get into the woods at the top of the climb before the man behind reached the drinks station I'd be out of sight.

I figured that my chasers would think I was fast by the way I'd flown effortlessly past them. If I could stay out of sight then everyone behind would have nothing to chase; they'd think I was long gone. I knew my running abilities alone were probably not good enough to get me a win, so I was about to play poker. This was my big bluff. If it went wrong I was in big trouble. I sprinted hard for the woods, using much more effort than I had originally intended on this section.

Gasping sounds blazed from my lungs as I cut through the thinning copse where the track finally levelled off. I hadn't dared look back on the climb, so I didn't know if my escape plan had worked. Easing off the gas, I let gravity pull me smoothly yet swiftly down the farm lane that led into the historic 'Plague Village' of Eyam.

In 1665, a parcel of cloth contaminated with disease-carrying fleas was delivered from London to an Eyam tailor. Within three days the tailor had died from the bubonic plague that was killing a huge number of London's population. It spread quickly through the village. In an attempt to stop it spreading to other villages, the inhabitants of Eyam adopted a self-imposed quarantine – nobody in, nobody out - knowing that for many of them it would be a death sentence. A third of the population died. Many families were wiped out. One resident, Elizabeth Hancock, buried her husband and six children in the space of eight days. But the valiant self-sacrifice saved the lives of many thousands living nearby. This astoundingly brave act has never been forgotten.

Another steep ascent out of the village, not far from the plague memorial, had me casting concerned glances over my shoulder. I'd thrown my cards on the table; I'd played my hand. I hadn't planned the race to go this way, but I had seen a weakness and attempted to exploit it. There was insufficient fuel in the tank to allow another fierce uphill effort *and* get me to the end, so I walked, watched and worried.

My card was out of my bum-bag pocket and ready to be stamped as I pottered into the first checkpoint at Eyam youth hostel. I needed to be in and out quickly, but the marshals weren't quite ready. I hurried them along and gulped down some water. After thanking them, I was left with the words of one lady marshal ringing in my ears, "You're doing really well. Only one person has been through in front of you". What! No! That couldn't be. I watched everyone leave at the start; I counted them all out and counted them all back. There was nobody in front of me.

Was there?

This was unsettling, but I had no choice but to press on regardless. I was gasping once again as the radio mast on the summit of the Sir William Hill came into close view. This was the highest point of the route, and now came a high speed plummet down a tricky moorland path to the valley bottom. This wasn't a good time to lose concentration. I put any concerns out of my mind and remembered my chaser's weakness. I flew down like a madman, trying to extend any lead I may have had, if I had any at all.

I was quick to get hidden under the cover of trees again, this time for the long, easy climb up Abney Clough. This required a conservative speed, but being at the front gave me the advantage of getting a clear passage over the muddy trail. I could see where the firmest footsteps were. By the time a few runners had passed, the trail would be far more churned up and slippery.

Checkpoint two was located in the hamlet of Abney, and this time they were ready. My card was stamped, two cups of water drunk, and a couple of biscuits grabbed to nibble on the next leg. I had to ask, "How many runners have been through?"

"None, You're the first".

That was a relief, but at the same time it was a curse. I hadn't expected to be in any position to win the race, and now the pressure was on me to stay in front, with an awfully long way to go.

Abney was the northern turnaround point of the route. From there the trail doubled back and was mostly on open fields and moorland. There was nowhere to hide. As I jogged and munched on the biscuits I kept a keen eye on the hill that I had just flown down half to my left. There was nobody descending it. "Damn, that must mean they are closer than I thought", I worried, "just in the valley close to Abney." But I was wrong.

The next steep climb, out of Bretton Clough, felt like an ascent of Everest. Leaning forward and pushing on my thighs with both hands, I once again tried to escape chasing eyes. As the gradient lessened and the track turned to the right I dared to look behind - and there was a runner. He wasn't breathing down my neck, though. I estimated him to be eight minutes behind as he ran through the fields before plummeting down into Bretton Clough. But had he seen me? Surely my white t-shirt shone like a beacon on the hillside, so I had to assume that he had. What was he thinking? Was I too far away to chase, or close enough to try to run down?

I had an easy, steep downhill on a road before a flat mile to Housley. I did some mental arithmetic, deciding that I should be well over a mile ahead and out of sight before the chaser got to Bretton ridge. But we weren't half way round yet.

Checkpoint three at Housley produced another quick stop, and then I began the mile-and-a-half climb through exposed fields to the top of Longstone Moor. Energy levels were starting to fade, and leg strength felt low as I passed the half way point. Another glance back from the top of the moor proved nothing; I couldn't see anyone but I daren't take the time needed for a good look.

The next downhill was lengthy, and would be the last one for several miles. My thigh muscles had taken a tough beating by the time I reined them in to stop me at checkpoint four in the village of Great Longstone. I had trained for downhill, worked at eccentric contractions and done tens of thousands of squats, but this was far more than they were used to. I was hammering down, trying to put time in the bank. This had started smoothly and easily, but now technique was fading, and every step felt like I had doubled in weight. How much more could my legs take?

Three miles of flat, disused railway line offered some respite, but also brought numerous nervous backward glances. I attempted some more mental arithmetic, but clear thinking was becoming cloudy, a sign that blood sugar levels were dropping. I knew the advantage of knowledge rested with my chaser – at each checkpoint he would know how many minutes behind me he was. He would know how quickly he was catching me and would be able to time his attack.

I figured that I still had a lead of a few minutes, and that a good runner on this course would steam along the railway line at less than seven minutes per mile. So I set that as my target, and kept checking my GPS unit. The pace was hard to maintain with legs that were pummelled by gravity, but I had played my bluff after the first hill and had to stick it out. The rate of fuel consumption was surely too great for the amount of energy left in the rapidly emptying tank. I was going for broke.

The end of the railway line dropped me onto a farm track that climbed gradually towards the penultimate hill. I had somehow reached 18 miles in a time ludicrously quicker than I'd intended. The unshielded sun punished me from its grandstand in space, scraping fluid from my bare skin and further dehydrating my arid body. This made chewing the biscuits I had carried from checkpoint five even harder. I needed the sugar and salt they contained, but struggled to swallow the mouthful of dry gravel. Walking had usurped running on anything other than downhill. Surely any moment I'd hear footsteps and fast breathing racing from behind as I crashed into second place, then third, fourth...

The steep track down into Rowsley proved to be more a bounce than a run, my body increasingly resembling a pinball hammering between the bumpers. Feet bashed from stone to stone, ankles wobbled, knees buckled, and my upper body shook jerkily.

Mile 20 was where the bonk first hit hard. Glycogen stores were empty, plundered, pillaged by rampaging running. No glycogen equals no speed. Fat reserves were forced to sail the sinking ship slowly towards the finish, but the waters over which I was sailing were far from calm. I hadn't taken time to drink enough at the checkpoints. Blood sugar levels were painfully low. The results were ghastly; a pounding head, aching limbs, muscle cramps, and feelings of nausea. But I was still winning. For the moment, anyway.

My legs dragged me up the last hill into Rowsley wood, and checkpoint six. Raging thirst tied me to the drinks table, and threatened to bind me there for the next hour. The desire to be the first to finish stole thirst's keys, unshackled me from the table and dragged me, wobbling, into the woods.

I'd had forgotten the sting in the tail of this race. The path turned up the side of a narrow river gorge, and pointed straight to heaven. My body felt like it was being sucked down into hell as I leaned into the slope and threw every sinew into clawing to the top of the muddy bank. I hauled myself across a sturdy wooden bridge above the cascading stream. Below it looked like paradise; I could have lain under the waterfall with my mouth open and allowed it all to gush into me, flooding me to a watery re-birth.

The gate at the end of the concrete pathway almost tripped me as I stumbled into the final checkpoint in Beeley village, unsure of how I'd made it down from the woods. I remembered how the sunlight had relit my darkening world as I popped out of the trees and looked down into the valley below. That was a mile back. What had happened in between?

The friendly marshals ushered me onwards with the words that sweetened my ringing ears like a cup of sugary tea. "Well done, only three miles to the finish".

Three miles. I was winning with three miles to go.

The path through Chatsworth Park was flat, following the floodplain of the river Derwent, and took an almost straight line through benign grassy fields. Benign was good. Anything with any menace would have finished me off. The first stretch was through a field packed with sheep, most of which were huddled in a tight group across the path. Sheep: benign.

Gears ground jerkily upwards from 'walk' into 'pained jog', and the flock began to part in front of me, like Moses crossing the Red Sea. As I approached the centre of the quietly scattering mass, one animal didn't move. The mountainous ram, around which all the ladies had been cooing, stood motionless, posturing at me with its head down, chest puffed out and feet planted widely and solidly; unmovable. Two black-hole eyes stared threateningly, projecting a message with the clarity of a fifty-foot billboard: "Not moving!" Benign?

200 pounds of solid, testosterone-fuelled, four-legged animal surrounded on its own territory by its mates versus 160 pounds of exhausted, bonking, two-legged wobbly idiot was a contest I knew I couldn't win. (The ram and I were both bonking that day, but in different contexts of the word!) I took a detour to the left, giving the beast at least twenty metres of space. All the while it never moved, not a muscle, not an eyeball. It stared menacingly back up the path from whence I'd run, sending another message, this time to his flock. "See that, ladies? Who's the daddy?" He was.

Suffering terribly with every step, I dare not let up the pace. Running was by now totally out of the question. Walking was painful. A pattern of jog/walking was possible, but that was wringing every last ounce out of what I was capable. The bottom of the fuel barrel had been scraped long back, and now I was hacking at the barrel itself and throwing the chippings onto the fading fire.

Was I still out of sight? Every time I looked back there were people, lots of people walking through the grounds of the massive estate. I had no idea whether one or more of them were chasing me. If they were I wouldn't have been able to do anything about it. They would beat me for sure. To lose it now would be too hard to take. I had to run myself into the dirt.

The distance markers on my GPS had gone into super slow-motion. I couldn't hold a straight line. The headache and dizziness were wrestling for attention with the uncontrollable legs. There was no doubt I was going to run myself into the dirt; it was simply a question of whether I'd make it as far as the dirt at the finish.

That was in serious doubt when I looked at my GPS as it beeped for the end of the 24th mile. The picture my eyes were sending to my brain began to darken and spin, black rings closed around the edges, and I was staring into hazy and dimming tunnel vision. There was just one mile to go and I was going to fade away into a hypoglycaemic collapse. I needed sugar, and quick.

What an idiot! It suddenly struck me; I had the gel sachet in my bumbag. Weak, shaky hands spun the waist strap and fumbled at the zip. The gloopy orange gel tasted better than the best thing ever. Why the hell hadn't I used it several miles back? It may had just given me enough of a kick to have reached the finish by now. I would have won. But swallowing it now would only make me feel a little bit better. The fuel wouldn't get to my legs until after I had reached Baslow.

What the gel did do was slap me across the face and turn some lights on in the visual tunnel. I wasn't moving any faster than I had been before I ate it, but at least I was still moving and not lying waiting for an ambulance. I made a mental note to self: don't run with calories in your pocket when you need them in your body.

The over-shoulder glances had increased in frequency to roughly one every five seconds as I spun open the rotating iron gate that links Chatsworth Park with Baslow. Determination was now driving the machine, and it was a merciless commander, putting its foot down hard on the gas to power a final sprint to the finish, fuelled on grit and God-knows-what and doing God-knows-what damage to my body.

I stumbled through the door of the village hall, bumped into two chairs on my way to the register's desk, and slapped my card on his table.

A ripple of applause spread weakly through the startled ensemble of marshals, helpers and tea ladies.

I had finished. In four hours and two minutes. First!

But the nightmare certainly hadn't finished.

***

I plonked myself down on the nearest chair, my body on fire with a cocktail of satisfaction and self-destruction. The few other people in the room transmitted a cheery atmosphere, and insisted on chatting to me, oblivious to the signals that I was transmitting that screamed "Leave me alone to die". I was imploding into the worst bonk I had ever experienced.

Muscles were screaming for calories, brain and blood were howling for fluids, but the stomach fought viciously with solid and aggressive resistance. The first cup of tea tasted like nectar, but went down with difficulty and sat heavily, threatening a return trip. A cup of sweet orange squash lay on top of it, trying to provide stability. One of the beaming cooks wandered over and asked if I'd like my pie and peas now, or would I prefer to wait. What the hell? I thought. Pile it in. And all the time I stared at the door, waiting for my chaser to sprint in the room.

The pie was piping hot, and I inflicted yet more self-harm by burning the skin on the roof of my mouth. More orange squash added to the concoction churning inside a stomach that had been starved of blood flow for the last four hours. Vomiting became a likely outcome. Feeling it would be bad manners to throw up the lovingly prepared victuals inside the hall, I staggered out to a quiet corner of the car park and lay face down on the tarmac, my thumping pounding head in my hands, palms squashing face.

And there I stayed for a quarter of an hour, until the desire for sugar grew stronger than the urge to be sick. 'Beaming cook' greeted me as I ambled back inside, "Ooh, love, are you feeling any better? You looked rough out there." I just raised my eyebrows at her, shook my head and blew out a very long and very deep sigh. I was still the only finisher. I sat down, drinking more tea and stuffing in pieces of cake, watching the door with a sense of disbelief.

Second finisher ran into the room, with third place hot on his heels. I checked the clock; it was a full 28 minutes after my damaging sprint finish that now had been so obviously, ludicrously unnecessary. 28 minutes. I could have walked from the Beeley checkpoint and still finished first. I had been convinced I was going to be caught, but ever since the first downhill I had been ripping away like a missile. And, just like a missile I had exploded. But I had won by 28 minutes.

I sat for another hour, pouring in fluids, stuffing down cake and biscuits, and chatting to other competitors as they trickled through the finish. Eventually the time came to go back home. Legs still complained noisily as I wandered back towards the rotating iron gate that led back into Chatsworth, and to where the car was parked. Two runners passed in the opposite direction, duelling to the finish, and I gave them a shout of "Good running".

There were five missed calls and three text messages on my mobile phone as I pulled it from the glove compartment of the car. Andrea was worried. She had been expecting a call to say I'd finished safely, but I hadn't had my phone with me. I called straight back and got an earful of concern. After I explained the events she was happy; it had simply been not knowing that had troubled her.

I pulled my jogging trousers back on to keep warm, and then pulled off my white t-shirt and threw it onto the back seat. It had become my 'lucky' white t-shirt. I'd wear it for every important event from now on.

***

How?

'How' is the second question ultra-distance runners are asked: how *do* you run that far?

There is no doubt that the human body is able to withstand

tremendous physical punishment, as the resilience and recovery shown by Andrea throughout her prolonged and sustained onslaught at the hands of her cancer treatment clearly demonstrate.

If we can take *that* abuse, then a long run in the hills should be no more than a walk in the park. All we need is the determination to endure. And it is then a simple case of one step at a time.

We are built from the right stuff to run ultra-marathons, we just need to tune the machine. Put in the right physical training, and seemingly impossible distances become possible. But you have to believe that you *can* do it. Without that belief you'd never get to the start line. Psychological training is as essential as the physical; you have to work on the belief.

Both these factors are closely linked. The more you train and the better the training progresses, the more self-belief you develop. And the more you believe, the better you train. A positive spiral rapidly emerges.

I knew this to be true, but I found myself asking another 'why'. Why, even with training and a confident, positive attitude, did my recent runs always seem to end the same way? I always made it to the finish, but ended up grinding myself into a bonking mess in the process. Why?

It hadn't been the best year for training, but I was well prepared for Chatsworth. However, the blueprint for the sensible pacing of that race was torn up on the first downhill. With hindsight, my pace throughout the Lyke Wake was also too fast for the conditions. Inappropriate fluid and calorie intake during these runs also contributed to the nauseating bonk.

I had learned an essential lesson that I could take forward to the New York marathon. Stick to a planned, sensible pace, and drink and eat sensibly. That's the way to avoid a mammoth bonk and all its associated unpleasantness.

Be sensible.

***

October saw Andrea's first follow-up appointment with Dr Purohit since finishing treatment. Physically she was feeling good, growing in strength and life was returning to its pre-cancer normality, and Dr Purohit was happy. The surgical scar was healing nicely, and radiation burns had long since disappeared. The writhing gastric worms of chemotherapy nausea were a distant memory.

But she was still troubled by the psychological aspects that the disease had inflicted. Dr Purohit was once again asked to explain the chances of a full and permanent recovery. Honey and gravel combined to repeat that the chances were good, but there were no certainties. Statistics, probability and hope: that was where the answer lay.

At the end of October the postman handed me a small cardboard box. I carried it into the living room and stared at it in quiet excitement for a minute before slowly slicing the sealing tape and carefully unwrapping the contents. As I lifted the lid the light shone eagerly on to the spines of ten books, all aligned the same way, and all smiling back at me. Down the length of each spine were the words *Coast To Coast*, and printed below those words was my name.

My journal of the run across the country had expanded and evolved, outgrown its pretence to be a mere diary, and now sat on my lap as a published book. The front cover showed a fantastic picture, taken by Vin, of my rear end as I jogged along the southern bank of Ennerdale Water in the Lake District. I had written a book. It wasn't huge, and would never win any prizes for literature, but it was definitely a book. Where on earth had I found time to do that?

Searching for it on Amazon sent my heart racing. There it was, for sale to the whole world. I was amazed, and even more amazed when it began collecting five-star reviews. People were buying it, and liking it.

Just days later Andrea and I climbed aboard the plane to New York, and headed to finish what had been an immensely testing year with a few days of careless togetherness. We flew high above the world, feeling like we were on top of it and watching it spin steadily from dark into light, reflecting the quantum shift through which our lives had passed. We were heading for bright lights, and hoped things stayed that way.

***

Boom, bump

Roadworks slowed the convoy of buses to a staccato crawl as we approached the Verrazano Narrows Bridge. Two lanes had to merge into one, and I looked out of the window on my left and into the coach full of marathon competitors alongside us. Some chatted, some dozed, each preparing themselves in their own way. There was no traffic other than the marathon convoy heading to the start area on Staten Island. With a lurch our bus moved forward through the cones, slowly at first, then faster and into second gear, and there was a deep booming noise followed by a long rumble, and the sunlight disappeared as we growled onto the bottom deck of the massive bridge.

The Verrazano Narrows Bridge, named after the Italian explorer Giovanni da Verrazzano, was an awe-inspiring site. Two decks carrying eight lanes of traffic arced dramatically over the Lower New York Bay, connecting the boroughs of Staten Island and Brooklyn. For seventeen years it was the largest single span suspension bridge in the world. Two huge towers shot hundreds of feet upwards, visible from all five New York boroughs, so tall and far apart that the curvature of the earth had to be considered in the design. The bridge would provide the first and largest hill of the marathon race as the 39,000 runners pounded their way back towards Brooklyn.

A glance through the window on the other side of the bus told me we were a giddy-making height above the river, and climbing steadily. The journey was still slow but there was no hurry. The Staten Island ferry could be seen in the distance, steaming down the Upper Bay, transporting thousands more entrants to the start. The ferry was the only other means of getting from Manhattan to the marathon start area; its five mile journey past Ellis and Liberty Islands would easily be quicker than the bus. Another judder and we moved forward once more, this time continuing at a crawling pace to the other side.

At the southern end of the bridge the athlete's village on Staten Island sprang into view. An immense area of parkland swarmed with people, walking, standing at food bars, or just sitting on the grass. Piercing sunlight blasted through the glass as the bus exited the bridge's lower tier, causing me to squint and shield my eyes with my hand. We trundled onto a wide area of tarmac, at the far end of which proudly stood a row of booths that formed the Verrazano Narrows toll barrier. It had the appearance of a row of battlements, standing solid against the invading army of athletes. This was the end of the ride. A marathon official jumped onto the bus, and in a mega-phonic American voice instructed us to disembark and head through the gates into the athlete's village, making sure to display our race numbers, without which entry would not be permitted.

The huge holding area filled a large acreage of Fort Wadsworth, a military installation that was first developed in 1663 as an ideal location to defend The Narrows. Its present name was adopted in 1864 to honour Brigadier General James Wadsworth, who had been killed in the Battle of the Wilderness during the American Civil War. On marathon day the only people allowed in were the competitors, a swarming human surge, herded *en masse* through the huge gates by the megaphones. "Keep moving! No stopping! Show your number!" It was as if Fort Wadsworth had turned into a military prison, and we, the inmates, were checked-in, homogenised and stripped of any individuality outside that of being a runner. Once inside there was no escape, no early release, and no time-off for good behaviour. The only way out would be across the start line and through 26.2 miles of hard labour.

Through the bottleneck of the main gates the crush of the herd eased and the tide of participants walked cheerily down the driveway towards one of three colour-coded areas. Multilingual banter filled the air, and I let the happy sounds wash over me without listening to anything in particular. In a way it reminded me of the joyful harmonious birdsong that resounded through my local woods during summer's evening training runs. Ahead and to the right I could see a large green archway constructed from hundreds of party balloons, gently swaying in the light morning breeze. That was my designated start area. Similar blue and orange arches highlighted the other areas. I was once again asked to show my race number to gain access. Lifting the front of my hoodie revealed the smart bib displaying the number 3873 in bold green lettering. The security official smiled and nodded. I had arrived.

The green area was adjacent to the bridge. Sizeable grassy parkland filled the gap between entrance and the massive structure, some 150 metres away, and stretched much farther up a slight rise to the left. I walked a few steps forward and took stock. I had still to fix my timing chip to my shoe, and decided to do it now. Finding a space I placed my bag on the ground and pulled out the small orange disc that was about the size of a fifty-pence piece, but twice as thick and with a hole at opposite sides. With it were provided two small orange tie-wraps. I placed the chip over my left forefoot, threaded the tie-wraps through the laces and fastened them securely.

The timing chip was a useful piece of technology that would register as I crossed sensors placed at the start and finishing lines. The race computer would record the exact timing of these events. In addition, the chip would register as I ran over sensors placed every five kilometres, and also at the 13.1-mile half marathon point. This system prevents the huge number of runners from pushing and jostling for position as they attempt to get over the start line, and ensures all competitors run against their own personal clock.

An added benefit at the New York Marathon was a feature called 'Athlete Alert'. The chip timing information could be sent by email. I had never come across this feature before, and was interested to see how well it worked. We planned to use it to our advantage. After her breakfast, Andrea was going to watch the race from the roadside on Manhattan's First Avenue. To give her some idea of when I would be passing that point I had specified Mal's home email address as one of my alerts. Mal would keep checking his computer and send text messages to Andrea, informing her of my progress.

I decided to go and explore the green area. Straight ahead I could see a narrow, roped-off tarmac lane, divided onto sections. Each section was labelled according to race numbers. The fastest competitors would start at the front and the slowest at the back. Curious to know where my estimated finishing time of three hours and fifteen minutes would put me in the line I found the corral labelled 3000 - 4000, and was delighted to see that it was the second from front section.

The corrals were closed, preventing entry until much nearer start time. Looking around, I could see there was more to discover, and top of my list was finding the free food stalls. Back across the grass, which was steadily filling with competitors, stood a stage on which a band enthusiastically blared out quality rock music to the massing hordes. There was nobody dancing; energy conservation was everyone's top priority. Next to the stage was a white medical tent. I peeped through the open doorway. Inside were several trestle tables on which stood an array of sticking plasters, and 'lollipop stick' applicators with a blob of Vaseline or similar product on the end. There was nothing I needed in there, so I wandered further up the field.

From behind the stage I could see a slight hill sloping upwards towards a long line of UPS vans, all parked side by side, and facing away with their back doors open. This was the bag drop area; the vans would be taking our belongings to the finish. Nearer was a concrete yard, around the edge of which were numerous stalls with the occupants handing out food and drink. Freebies! Now this seemed worth a look. I headed that way.

On the other side of the lane and across a thin strip of grass was the longest line of portable toilets I had ever seen (and having been to some big bike races in the past I had seen some *long* lines of toilets.) All of them dark blue, all facing exactly the same way, and all equally spaced as if positioned by a perfectionist portable-toilet technician with obsessive-compulsive disorder. I never imagined I'd think such a thing, but that line of toilets was almost a thing of beauty, a work of art. Damian Hirst could have put his name to it and sold it for a six-figure sum. Thinking of Hirst made me wonder whether formaldehyde was used in the chemical tanks. The line would make the perfect partner to his work *"beautiful revolving sphincter, oops brown painting"*. I suspected I'd be using one of the toilets in the near future, but became concerned that doing so would spoil their aesthetic appeal.

Extending from the near corner of the yard and winding down the hill was a queue of people. A queue! Being English I couldn't resist the overwhelming temptation to go and join it. It was disappointing to find it was a very slow moving queue. We do love a good queue, but only if they move at a satisfactory pace. My first thought was that it was the line of people waiting to get into the freebie area, but closer inspection showed that there was free access through the right hand side of the yard. I studied the queue further, which had by now extended twenty or so people behind me, and found it was only for the Dunkin' Donuts and coffee stall. This wasn't for me, I didn't want donuts or coffee, I wanted a nice, fast moving queue, and I resolutely overrode my English tendencies and extracted myself from the growing line of caffeine enthusiasts. As I did so, I felt the need to mumble something barely audible to nobody in particular, as if both an explanation and an apology for abandoning my place in the line. Why do we do that?

The stalls were all busy with runners accepting freebies. Staff stood behind tables, and behind them more staff pulled goods out of boxes and reloaded the tables as fast as they were emptied. Although there were sufficient supplies in my bag I took a bottle of water and a bagel, and then decided it was time to sit, rest and relax.

Alongside the yard was a grassy bank that sloped ten feet down to the lane. The aspect faced the sun, which was doing its best to disperse the chill as it slowly crept upwards, peeping through the giant cables that curved downwards and along the bridge from the massive southern tower. There was little room on the bank, it proving a popular place to try and catch some warming rays, but I found a spot, made myself as comfortable as I could and pulled the hood back over my head and face for warmth.

The bagel was pleasant, but proved difficult to eat *au naturel*. I'm a big fan of bagels, toasted with butter and marmalade or peanut butter, but this one proved too doughy and ended up being stuffed to the bottom of my bag. The bank was becoming overcrowded and was too steep to sit on comfortably. The grass on the other side of the road was far emptier, but still mostly shaded. Comfort trumped warmth, and I strolled over, found a nice flat area under a tree, plonked my bag down and lay next to it.

The ground and still air were colder than I expected, making my breath steam slightly, but I was comfortable and felt able to relax and concentrate on keeping calm. With eyes closed, and one end of my bag as a pillow, I switched off mentally and took some deep, slow breaths. My heart rate slowed, and serenity flowed through my relaxed body. An unhurried smile evolved from the tranquillity, and I felt happy, euphoric even, as if transported to another world somewhere inside myself, absolutely distant from the bustle all around.

***

I'm not sure how long I was asleep, but a chilled feeling brought me to my senses. It could only have been a few minutes, but in that time the grassy area became busier with relaxing runners. A constant hum filled the air, the source of which was a helicopter droning back and forth over the northern end of Staten Island. I opened my eyes, but didn't move. The sun had finally risen above the bridge and I was no longer in shade, although the cold was stubbornly refusing to leave. This seemed a good opportunity to do some stretching to warm me up as well as prepare my muscles for the impending marathon. Ever observant, I saw there was now a small queue of about half a dozen people in front of each toilet.

Queues!

It was inevitable that I had to go and join one, but which one? I took a gamble. It was also inevitable that I began the activity of looking at all the other queues to see how fast they were moving. Bloody typical! I was in the slowest queue.

A one-in-50 chance of picking the wrong one and I had done it. The psychological battle began. Do I leave this queue to join the back of another one, only to risk waiting longer and looking an idiot, or do I stick it out and hope that my queue bucks its ideas up and gets moving? And what are they doing in that toilet that was taking so long anyway? I tried not to ponder that question too much. The decision was made to stick with the same queue. Eventually I was at the front, standing ten yards from the door, and trying for decency's sake to look anywhere but at the cubicle itself.

Every time someone emerged from one of the other toilets the door swung shut, making a resonating drum-like booming sound, before bouncing slightly open again and shutting finally with a quieter bump. BOOM, bump! Someone exited two cubicles to the right. BOOM, bump! Then three to the left: BOOM, bump.

Once I noticed it I could focus on nothing else. One to the right: BOOM, bump! Three to the right: BOOM, bump!

BOOM, bump! BOOM, bump! BOOM, bump! Bloody BOOM, bloody bump!

The guy behind me tapped me on my shoulder. I had become so entranced by the percussive effects of a gazillion portable toilet doors shutting that I didn't see my cubicle become free. I apologised and stepped forward, gently closing and locking the door behind me. Now I could see why the queues were moving slower than expected. Portable toilets are not renowned for their comfort, cleanliness and generally pleasant ambience. The malodorous nature normally encourages rapid use and rapid exit. However, these toilets were now in sunshine, and the dark coloured plastic from which they were constructed had turned them into mini-ovens. It was pleasantly warm in there. The thermal benefits outweighed the unpleasant aroma.

After washing my hands I took a bit of time to apply 'chafe

protection'. Vaseline was smeared on my inner thighs (modesty and the fear of arrest prevented me from doing this whilst lying on the grass in full view in American recreational parkland) and I also lifted my vest, hoodie and jacket and stuck on nipple guards. Now safe from vicious rubbing effects I stood enjoying the warmth, and wondering whether to feign some nasty bowel condition so that I could stay in the toilet until the race started. This seemed an extreme measure, and the thought occurred to me that I was standing in a plastic box that contained a large tub of urine, excrement and unpleasant chemicals (Hirst's formaldehyde perhaps) that were being steadily heated by the sun. Very soon it would get decidedly unpleasant in here.

I peeped through the grill that was situated just above the door to provide basic ventilation and saw that the other runners in 'my' queue were starting to look somewhat impatient, the ones at the front staring harshly back at the toilet. The ones at the back were no doubt experiencing the 'should I change queues' dilemma. I felt that I had overstayed my welcome. As I exited I let the door go and it swung shut. BOOM, bump! Yeah! That was my contribution to the New York City marathon drum-and-*waste* musical extravaganza.

My previously occupied space near the tree was still free, so I went back, lay down and did some more stretching whilst trying to stay relaxed. Taking long, slow, deep breaths I tried to imagine myself running swiftly but comfortably through the undulating road through Central Park to the finish area, tens of thousands of spectators cheering. I had jogged the route of the last three miles on Friday morning with the tour group with whom Andrea and I had travelled. This had been a very useful exercise, despite it requiring me to get up early the morning after we had arrived in New York. As a bunch we jogged from the Crowne Plaza Hotel, up Broadway to the southern end of Central Park, led by Mike Gratton (the winner of the 1983 London Marathon) and his team.

That had been my first real experience of New York. And what an exciting, bewildering and magical experience it was too. The buildings in Midtown Manhattan seemed impossibly huge, almost as high as the mountains on which I usually ran. The sun shone its hardest, battling to get its piercing rays through the skyscrapers to the bustling madness on the pavements below, where innumerable people commuted and jostled along the sidewalks, coats pulled up high around necks to repel the November chill, paper cups of steaming coffee carried by many. Yellow taxis flashed by, horns hooted, people shouted the shouts of a million languages. Street vendors steamed the air with delicious scents of their cooking victuals. Monstrous neon billboards flashed, the ground rumbled with a passing subway train. Noise, colour, smells, people, lots and lots of people.

And through all the Big City madness jogged a cluster of runners, weaving in and out of the mayhem, darting across roads to avoid being run down by the incessant traffic, and trying to avoid collisions with the native populace heading in the other direction. It was a deliciously exciting new experience, and it felt like we were joyriding through an unfamiliar world and trying to run to freedom. I loved it. The words of Sting's song looped around my head as we jogged - "I'm an alien, I'm an Englishman in New York".

Mike Gratton showed us the end section of the race, which had several small, rolling bumps that were not large enough to be called hills. However, he warned us not to underestimate the impact these would have at the end of 26 miles of running. They didn't look big or bothersome to me, especially compared to those in the Peak District and the North York Moors that I had regularly battled. Mike's advice was to "keep some energy in reserve for the last five miles, because you'll need it". In honesty, I was more concerned that the course was too flat.

Mike's team ran us through the short rising section that led to the finish line, flanked on either side by temporary grandstand seating. The finish gantry and timing clock were already in place, giving the area a sense of mounting excitement. The atmosphere was slightly tense but also thrilling, like waiting to go to an enormously anticipated party. Many groups of runners were doing a similar thing and the park was bustling and lively with colour and energy. As we passed through the finish area a large crowd of Dutch competitors sat almost filling one section of the grandstand. All dressed in orange, they swayed from side to side singing a song while someone filmed them with a video camera. Further round on our jog we met the Dutch again. This time they were amongst the trees, all performing the same stretching routine, and all still singing the same song.

Thoughts of the Dutch made me laugh to myself, and I wondered if many of them were with me here in the green area. The tension was rising, and three helicopters now circled overhead, increasing the noise from the sky. One had the markings of the Police Department, whilst another was painted bright red and sported the livery of the Coastguard. Much higher flew an airship, advertising a television channel by means of a giant TV screen on its side – bizarrely, 'Homer Simpson' stared down at me from 500 feet.

With half an hour to the start I had to decide what to take with me. I had my small bum-bag that I could fill with energy bars, a small drink, and my jacket. Alternatively I could go without the jacket and risk being cold, and carry some energy bars or gels in my hand. There was no sign of any cloud and, although it was still cold, I suspected I would warm up quickly as the running got underway. There were also drink stations *en route* every mile after the fourth, so there was no need to carry water. I decided to leave the jacket behind and run as light as possible.

My hydration level was good. So good in fact that I had to go and play toilet queue roulette once again, with all its associated BOOM, bumping. Before taking my bag to the UPS van I took out my GPS device, and switched it on to give it time to get a fix on my position. I wasn't sure how well it would work on the streets of New York, as large buildings can block the satellite signals. But I was used to running with it and thought it could be very useful to help maintain my planned running speed.

I went through one last mental checklist: Shorts, lucky shirt, socks, shoes with timing chip fitted? Yep, wearing those under my hoodie and baggy trousers. Contact lenses in, nipple guards on and vaseline'd up?

Yep! GPS on my wrist, two gel sachets in my hand, and a bottle of water to drink until the start? Check!

Everything seemed in order. I was ready, and strolled nervously over to the line of vans, found the one labelled with '3000 – 4000' and handed over my bag of worldly goods. I now had nothing other than what I was wearing until I reached the finish in Central Park. It never occurred to me at the time, but I had absolutely no idea what to do if I were forced to abandon the race for some reason. How the heck would I get back? How would I get my belongings back, and how would Andrea know where I was?

The Tannoy system announced, in several languages, that the race would soon be starting and all athletes should make their way to their allotted corral. As if a giant stick stirred up the human ant nest once again, activity increased all around. I casually jogged the hundred yards across the grass towards my corral. I wanted to keep moving and loosen up yet avoid expending unnecessary energy. The rope across the corral entrance had been removed and replaced by a security marshal who was again checking race numbers to ensure they entered the right section. I took the opportunity for one more good stretch on the field before revealing my number once again. There was another portable toilet inside the corral, and a number of fit, athletic looking men (no women?) formed an exclusive mini-line for the BOOM, bump. One competitor lay sprawled on the grass verge in a corner, looking as though he was asleep. Or dead! Dark sunglasses covered his eyes, so it was impossible to be sure.

I found myself nervously checking-out all the other runners, in a kind of 'are-they-better-than-me-or-can-I-kick-their-ass?' manner. I doubt I was the only one undergoing this ludicrous alpha-male behaviour. Frankly, they *all* looked like they could kick my ass. Thankfully there were no fancy dress runners here. No Wombles, Rhinoceros, Mr Blobby or giant ducks. I wasn't going to head over the bridge desperately trying to keep up with a dozen blokes in a centipede outfit. Come to think of it, I hadn't seen *any* fancy dress runners at all in the green start. Maybe New

York just isn't that kind of marathon. Or maybe they were all in the orange or blue starts. I finished a small bottle of water and pondered the fancy dress issue while standing in the exclusive line of '3000 – 4000' marathon percussion BOOM bump boys.

The noise continued to rise, both on the ground and in the sky. The tannoy continued its multilingual instructions to head to the starting corrals which were rapidly filling. Ground sitting space had gone and there was little room for anyone else to get in the corral. Everyone was standing facing forward, resembling a massed army awaiting the order to charge its enemy.

The band on stage behind us thrashed out a lively rock song that didn't harmonise well with the music that had started to blast out from the start area near the tollbooths a hundred metres to my left. There were now four helicopters buzzing all over the music anyway, especially the police and coastguard, who repeatedly flew in and hovered low over the three developing giant human snakes – green, blue and orange. Behind and to the left a TV broadcast helicopter hung motionless above the bridge. Ahead and to the right flew a small aeroplane, pulling a banner on which was written something I couldn't read.

The music from the bridge stopped, only to be replaced by a muffled voice from loud speakers. Then a loud BANG split the air, and a tight cluster of runners could be seen charging up the top deck of the bridge, heading north towards Brooklyn. This was the start of the elite race – the professionals and super-quick athletes who set off a few minutes before the massed ranks of pavement pounders.

Ahead I could see people streaming out from the blue and orange starts, but walking not running. They were stopped again on the wide toll area. Then the front corral from my line was ushered forward, and the bunch in which I was standing started to amble after them. Sensing we'd be away at any second I pulled off my hoodie and threw it over the fence to my left. This was followed immediately by the baggy trousers I had been wearing, revealing a smart pair of 'Union Jack' running shorts that I had bought specially for this event. This brought comments from a couple of men who were standing next to me.

"Whoooo, nice shorts," said the first.

"Yeah, man," agreed his colleague. "You'll get lots of comments from the crowd wearing *those*."

The shorts certainly were striking, not only in the colourful design, but also because they were cut higher than I'd normally wear. They felt indecent, but looked good sandwiched between my tight, white, lucky running shirt and a pair of white ankle socks that peeped above bright white and blue trainers. The only thing that spoiled the colour co-ordination was the orange timing chip sitting conspicuously on my left foot.

At that moment the forward momentum ceased, and we were standing still again. I'd removed my warm clothes too early, and the morning chill brought goose bumps to my bare arms and legs. I looked longingly at my discarded clothes on the other side of the fence. There was no way I could get them back. After a minute of shivering I adopted the penguin tactic and slowly eased into the middle of the group to keep warm.

My discarded hoodie and trousers were a tiny part of a huge, and growing, assortment of clothing that was steadily raining over the fence from thousands of competitors who were stripping-off. We wouldn't get this clothing back. It would all be collected by charitable services and handed out to the homeless people of New York. I'd grown to like my rapper outfit. I hope whoever became the beneficiary liked them too.

It wasn't long before we were herded forward towards the bridge and joined the heaving throng, all champing at the bit to get going like the excited mass of horses and riders at the start of the Grand National, only a thousand times more numerous. The man with the loudspeaker energised the crowd still further with more well-chosen words (although again I couldn't tell what he said). Then another loud bang rang out, followed this time by a huge cheer. The floodgates were releases, and a tidal wave of multinational athleticism surged onto the bridge (although I assume that at the back it was more of a trickle). The race had started.

More music blared from the speaker columns, this time I recognised 'Born in the USA' by Bruce Springsteen.

The pack around me were shuffling forwards, still 30 yards from the start line, then fast walking, then jogging, and then there it was, the red carpet over the sensor that would register my first step of the 26.2 mile trip towards Manhattan. Beeps rapidly and repeatedly filled the air with a chirruping sound as each runner's chip passed over the sensor, sounding like a thousand Morse Code messages all arriving at once. I have no idea which beep was mine, but it sounded just as Bruce Springsteen sang the words "You end up like a dog that's been beat too much". Did he know something I didn't? I pressed the start button on my GPS unit and set off. Central Park, here we come.

***

The Wall

The corral system had worked well, and I was delighted to be running at my own pace and not crowded-in. Both decks of the Bridge were being used for the race. The 'green' start runners were directed onto the lower deck, and I found myself running back up the carriageway that the bus had driven down. The excitement and anticipation of the athlete's village had rapidly evaporated to be replaced by an atmosphere of business-like running.

There was almost a silence, an eerie quietness suffocated by rhythmic heavy breathing and thousands of feet patting the concrete. A sublime, almost unnoticeable, rumbling could be felt as the giant structure resonated to the percussion of millions of foot-strikes. In front of me stretched the narrow strip of freeway, curving ever so slightly upwards. Thousands of heads bounced above brightly coloured running vests. The upper deck and the vertical supports of the bridge framed the image like I was inside a wide-screen TV. It was somehow a beautiful illustration of man and the manufactured in a fantastic aesthetic. I imagined the scene would be repeated on the top deck, only here the outside world would be able to view the spectacle via the pictures transmitted from the helicopters. I felt privileged to be a part of it.

I glanced to the left and peered down the hundreds of feet to the river. The New York fireboat was in the middle of the channel, spraying jets of water high in all directions from its powerful hoses. The angle of the sun was perfect, and a vivid rainbow hovered alongside the vessel, adding nature's colour to the extravaganza. A long way upstream stood the Statue of Liberty, saluting us with her proudly raised torch, and a little further north the skyscrapers of Manhattan jabbed at the clear blue sky, which had such clarity it seemed impervious to the invasion.

I reminded myself not to get carried away with the poetic. There was a race to be run. A marathon is too far to run to the best of your ability without maintaining concentration. Allowing the quiet to help me, I refocused. My target running pace was seven minutes 25 seconds per mile - too fast and I'd run the risk of 'hitting the wall' in the later stages. Too slow and I'd be unlikely to make up lost time. Unfortunately there was no signal for my GPS receiver on the bottom deck of the bridge, rendering it useless. I was relying on running by feel for the first two miles, settling into a comfortable rhythm, keeping my breathing steady, and moving in a smooth, flowing manner. What I could do was look out for the marker that signified the end of the first mile, and check the time on my stopwatch. In the throng I recognised the two guys who had commented on my shorts, and eased my way across to them. We exchanged greetings and good-luck wishes before splitting again. During this brief chat I missed the first mile marker.

The slight downward slope of the north side of the bridge pulled me onwards, and I was flowing. I flowed out from the bottom deck onto Interstate 278 and into bright Brooklyn sunlight. The two-mile marker sprang into view and I checked my stopwatch. It read thirteen minutes 30 seconds, well over a minute faster than planned. I wasn't flowing, I was gushing. This was too fast. I knew I should slow down, but the pace just felt so comfortable, almost effortless. My breathing was light and gentle, and everything felt easy. Surely I just needed to keep relaxed and everything would be all right? Surely!

A family stood watching from a bridge over the road. They had hung a sheet down with the words 'Welcome to Brooklyn' painted on it. Three children waved down at the runners. I waved back, and they cheered. Strangely, there were fewer people around than I had imagined. The green stream seemed alone. There weren't enough runners around to account for all 39,000 competitors. Looking over to my left, about a hundred metres away, I saw another street full of athletes. That was the orange stream. Then another wave of runners passed over us from right-to-left on a bridge that crossed the interstate. That was the third stream, blue.

We pulled off the highway and took a left turn into a residential street that was adorned on both sides by tall, old houses with domineering gable ends, reminiscent of *The Addams Family* or *The Munsters*. Adding to the impression, a few front yards still sported pumpkin lanterns and scary figurines that were a Halloween hangover. But the local residents who had ventured onto the sidewalk were far from scary - cheering, clapping, waving, and offering sweets and bananas to the invading masses.

The five-kilometre marker was announced by the audible multiple Morse Code madness, and I checked my watch. 21 minutes! I hadn't slowed down at all and was still going way too fast. Ahead I could see that at the end of the street we would take a sharp right turn onto a wider road, and pouring across the junction were the massed ranks of the two other streams.

I made the turn, and the sight was unbelievable. Brooklyn's 4th Avenue, a wide carriageway, was completely packed from sidewalk to sidewalk with a huge surge of runners, all pouring forwards at speed. It was the human equivalent of a stampeding herd of migrating animals; power, energy and determination channelled into one single-minded, focused goal; an unstoppable force, charging through the city like a tidal wave erupting from a dam-burst. On either side stood tremendous crowds of spectators. The noise was incredible.

Estimates suggest two million people take to the streets of New York to watch the marathon. As there are six miles of the course on spectator-free bridges, roughly 100,000 spectators per mile cram the sidewalks. They were shouting, cheering, clapping, blowing toy horns, and banging on the barriers over which they leaned. I had never known an atmosphere like it at a race. Children and adults alike were holding out their hands to be 'high-fived' by passing runners. Younger children sat on their father's shoulders, cheering and reaching out their tiny hands. In some places, rows of children stood in a line; all with outstretched arms, and it was possible to run past and high-five the whole line in one go.

Anything about a runner that singled them out from the masses was used to cheer them on. Many had their country's flag on their clothing. I heard yells of *"Meyheeeeco!"*, *"Eeeetalia, Eeeetalia!"*, *"Allez France!"* and *"Go,*

Italy, go!". Other runners had names printed on their shirts, and I heard *"Good job, Dave"*, and *"Way ta' go, Suzie"*. I was utterly enthralled by an atmosphere so sensational I got goose bumps, and the hairs on the back of my neck tingled.

The experience was hugely moving, but in a different way to the profound individuality of the long solo hilltop run. It was a different religion, a new one to me. This was collective euphoria. The combined energy and spirit of thousands of competitors multiplied, mingled, and transmitted through the atmosphere like a powerful subliminal emotion. I knew then why people entered mass participation events. It was like going to their church: I was among their congregation.

And the crowd were also important participants. They weren't running, but they received the energy, felt the passion, added to it and transmitted it back into the air all around. This was the biggest event of its type in the world. It was a pilgrimage that drew worshippers from all corners of the globe.

I had been running about ten feet from the right hand side of the road, but I wanted a piece of the crowd action. I was seeing, hearing and feeling the carnival, but I wanted to touch it as well. Gently I eased my way through to the right hand kerb, and was immediately rewarded with screams of *"Yeah England!"* and *"Go Brits!"* My shorts were attracting attention. Sometimes I'd see spectators waving Union Flags over the barriers in front of me, and I'd always make the effort to point and wave at them.

To have complete strangers cheer and wave my nation's flag at me was both exciting and emotional. I felt this must be what it was like to be a rock star. Although we were no more than ordinary runners from ordinary towns, to the people watching today we were their sporting idols. If I still had my hoodie and trousers on and stood next to them they wouldn't give me a second look, but running past in my Union Jack shorts they wanted to cheer me, to clap me, to be hi-fived by me. Hell, I may even have got a kiss or two.

I checked my pace on the GPS – six minutes 40 seconds per mile! My 'sensible' head was starting to get frustrated. My 'reckless' head, however, was having simply the best time running that it had done for ages. The two began to argue.

Sensible: Slow down!

Reckless: Yeeeeeeeeeee Haaaaaaaaaaaah!!!!!

Sensible: Never mind 'Yee Hah'. We've got to put the brakes on or we'll be in trouble before Manhattan.

Reckless: Whoop, whoop, whoop, *whooooooop*!

Sensible: Stop it now! I mean it. There's still a long way to go.

Reckless: Quit whining! This is great fun, and we feel terrific. There's no problem. Let's do some more high-fives. Hey, that guy just waved an England flag at us.

Sensible: SLOW DOWN!

Heart chipped in: Aw, give him a break, sensible. This is fantastic. I've just been chatting to *lungs* and we're not putting in much effort. We'll be fine.

Sensible: Well don't blame me when we crash and burn with miles still to run.

Reckless: Stop being such a sissy. *Tally-Hooooo*..........!!!!

At which point *Sensible* lurked off into the background and sulked, knowing he was right and that it would all end in tears. I ran on, aware that I should slow down, but I just couldn't do it.

In the Bay Ridge district the noise from the spectators was deafening. On a shop forecourt a band played a loud, and rather good, version of 'Waltzing Along' by the band James. In fact, there seemed to be bands playing at every street corner, and all musical tastes were catered for. There were rock bands, jazz bands, reggae outfits, rhythm and blues, and even Scottish bagpipes. It was a 26-mile long street party, a party to which the emergency services were invited. Fire trucks blocked side roads, and the fire fighters, dressed in uniform, shouted and waved. Some of them were in the bucket on the crane, lifted high above the runners.

And cops were everywhere. The criminals must have been having an easy day.

A large, black, female cop was standing holding her hand out in front of me. I raised mine to high-five her, and she enthusiastically swung her arm to meet mine. You could probably have heard the slap from the Bronx. She whacked my hand so hard she almost knocked me back to Staten Island. Another bunch of firefighters were standing by their truck, shouting and applauding. One of them yelled, "You're all heroes!"

Whoa there! Time out! If I could have paused time there and then, I would have done. Here was a man who worked for the New York Fire Department. On September 11th 2001 he and/or his colleagues raced *en masse* to downtown Manhattan and into the World Trade Centre. We all know what happened. The Fire Department lost many men that day, men who then risked their lives as routine. We, on the other hand, were out for a run. OK, many were raising significant amounts of money for worthy causes, but heroes? No! I wanted to stop and explain that we were merely runners - *they* were heroes. Un-pause...

The four-mile point arrived and there was a narrowing in the road caused by a drink-station. This produced a slowing in pace as runners weaved around and arranged themselves in the most appropriate position to grab a cup from the donors who stretched for 20 or 30 metres along the sides of the road. The volunteers were all dressed in matching green polythene raincoats. There were two choices of drink: Poland Spring water or Gatorade, a sweet lemon-lime flavour sports drink. I signalled my intention to a volunteer who held out a cup of Gatorade. We both prepared for the challenging act of transferring a paper cup, half filled with fluid, from a stationary point (the volunteer) to a moving object (myself) with maximum efficiency and minimum mess. This is not an easy task, and I would recommend that anyone wanting to see the funny side of a marathon should stand close to a drink station.

At a marathon drink station the cup of fluid has to go from zero to eight miles an hour in the space of two feet. And once it reaches that speed it is bounced up and down as the recipient attempts to run and drink at the same time. *This* is why the volunteers were all wearing raincoats, and why the cups were only half full. Drinks were being thrown into the air, drenching everything around, and cups were bouncing in all directions. The road around the station and for a hundred yards downstream was soaking wet and littered with discarded cups, many crushed flat beneath pounding feet. And I was very near the front of the race. What would the street look like by the time the 39,000th runner came past. They would be ploughing through a sticky, soggy, drenched paper-cup mountain. Perhaps this was why there were no Wombles running. There would be far too much 'Wombling' to do. By the time they'd have cleaned up all the litter at the first drink station the race would be over and everyone else would have gone home.

I grabbed the cup, and half the sticky drink sloshed over my hand and arm. I then tried to drink whilst I ran. This is usually something I do from a sports bottle, or my CamelBak, where there is a specifically designed mouthpiece. Sipping from a cup as you bounce along is just about impossible. A tiny fraction of the drink slops into your mouth in waves with each step. This erratic consumption provides too little fluid intake to be worthwhile, and dramatically disrupts your breathing. The great majority of the liquid jet-washes your face, splashes over your head and slops down the front of your shirt and shorts. The impromptu shower isn't much of a problem with water, but gloopy, sticky sports drinks don't make good coolant or body lotion. Some slopped into my right eye, causing me to blink and be concerned that my contact lens would get washed out. Thankfully, it didn't.

I decided enough was enough, dropped the cup to the floor and tried to regain my rhythm. I was still clutching the two gel sachets that I planned to consume later in the race, but now they were sticky and covered in Gatorade. In fact pretty much everything was sticky – my face, shirt, shorts, legs and right arm. I wondered if this could be of benefit. If I were to run out of energy later I could suck my clothes and lick my skin. Perhaps I should make more of an effort to cover myself in the drink at the next station. Perhaps not!

I was pleasantly warm now, and sweat was mixing with the tacky, drying Gatorade residue. It was an unpleasant feeling. Some spectators were holding out paper towels for runners to mop their sweat with. I took one at the first opportunity and wiped off as much spilt drink as I could.

The fantastic cavalcade continued for several miles as we rampaged north through the district of Sunset Park and towards Prospect Heights, heading to the borough of Queens. I was still feeling fantastic. But every single time I checked my GPS it told me I was going too fast.

At around the nine-mile mark the road took a 90-degree right-hand bend onto Lafayette Avenue, and went up a short but quite steep rise. The support was as fantastic as it had been earlier, but now the road seemed narrower and the crowd closer. This was the first time I felt any weakness in my legs. "No problem," I thought. "Just ease back on the pace up the hill and everything will be hunky dory." I'd planned to eat my gels at evenly spaced distances throughout the race, aiming to have one at nine miles and the other at eighteen miles.

Once over the brow of the little hill I ripped the top off the first gel sachet while keeping up with the river of runners that I could see bouncing onwards into the distance. I squirted the sweetly tasting jelly substance into my mouth, and it was good. It took three or four good squeezes on the packet to extract all its contents before throwing the empty container to the floor. I hate any kind of littering, and would be mortified to have done this under normal circumstances. But the marathon route was awash with sweet wrappers, banana skins (no slips that I saw), drinks bottles and empty gel sachets. An army of volunteers and trash collectors follow the race and sweep up any mess left behind.

The gel seemed to add a little zip to my general feeling and increase my alertness; the sudden hit of carbohydrate did its job. But I needed some water to go with it. That meant I had to run the gauntlet of the next drinking station / Gatorade shower / sticky bath. The ten-mile station was just around a left-hand bend on Bedford Avenue.

This time I aimed for the volunteers who were holding out cups of water, and this proved a far more pleasurable dousing. In fact I had become hot and the spontaneous soaking was nice. So nice in fact that after I had slurped a few random sloshes I tipped the rest over my head and placed the cup upside down on top of my soaking hair. I managed to run on a few steps, wearing the cup like a small white *fez* as the water trickled down my neck, much to the amusement of a watching police officer who laughed and shouted "*Way to go, England!*". Refreshed and still having a ball, the stampede sped on, following the East River towards Greenpoint district.

The desire to keep my blood sugar level high prompted me to do something my mother told me never to do. I took a sweet from a stranger. The elderly lady holding out the small, round, paper-wrapped confection looked friendly enough, and I was a big boy now and probably able to look after myself, so I risked it. I yelled a cheery "*thank you*" as I snatched the candy whilst running past. What harm could it do?

Well, quite a lot actually! I was expecting something soft and chewy, something easy to swallow, and something that would be gone in a few seconds. Instead the lady had tried to kill me with the hardest, toughest gobstopper I had ever eaten. It was the size of a marble, tasted nicely of strawberry, but it steadfastly refused to soften or break. Instead it became alive and aggressive in my mouth, and started playing a vicious game of oral pinball, bouncing around from one cheek to the other, smashing against my teeth, threatening to stick in my throat and then flying between my lips and producing chirrupy-whistling sounds as I fought for breath. Running became secondary to avoiding an untimely death by asphyxiation or internal head trauma.

The cannonball confection suddenly caught between my back teeth and I chomped hard. A loud cracking noise was followed immediately by shards of hard stuff blowing out of my mouth and onto the street. I wasn't sure whether the bits bouncing around on the tarmac were teeth or fragments of fruity wreckage, but frankly I didn't care. I had survived the elderly lady-sweet-toting terrorist attack and could get back to the serious businesses of waving and hi-fiving. Note to self: you should always do what your mum says. Never take sweets from strangers

One or two stubborn nuggets of sweet-debris remained lodged in my cheeks (I decided to leave them there for safety's sake) as the manic-Morse code beeps announced the crossing of the half-marathon point on McGuinness Boulevard. Another GPS check confirmed the persistence of my foolishness. I had just run the second fastest half-marathon of my life. Were I to stop now this would have been a good result; a performance I would be proud to write in my training logbook. But with the same distance still to run it was far too fast. My fate of a hideously painful end was now surely sealed.

Most people have heard of 'The Wall', a physical / psychological barrier that one hits metaphorically at about the 18-mile mark of a marathon race. Hitting the wall is simply another name for bonking. My reckless pacing was surely building a rather large and rather solid wall somewhere near Central Park. In my head *Sensible* mooched and sulked and contemplated heading for the lifeboats whilst *Reckless* and *Heart* waved, cheered, hi-fived and showboated, oblivious to the fact that their *Titanic* was steaming towards the iceberg.

Meanwhile, back in England, *Athlete Alert* was doing its job. Mal was checking his computer screen to find regular emails arriving from the marathon computer, telling him of each of my 5km split times. He could see my progress, and what great progress it was too. The half-marathon time flashed up, and he immediately sent a text message to Andrea, which read, "He's flying!" I *was* flying. Just like Icarus.

It's quite a story, but in Greek mythology Icarus and his father Daedalus were exiled in Crete by the King. Daedalus made two pairs of wings from feathers and wax to enable them to escape to freedom. Before they took off, Icarus was warned not to fly too close to the sun. But, overcome by the giddiness and excitement at being able to fly, Icarus soared high, and got too close to the sun. The heat melted the wax, and the feathers pulled off. Icarus plunged into the sea to his death (giving his name to the Icarian Sea). I, like Icarus, was flying, but my pace was far too hot. I was risking losing my wings before the end of the race.

After crossing the Pulaski Bridge a few bends twisted us further northwards to Long Island City, then a 90-degree left turn at Queensboro Plaza threw us onto the deck of the Queensboro Bridge for the mile-long crossing onto Manhattan. Suddenly there was silence once again, bar the foot slapping and heavy breathing.

The Queensboro Bridge, built in 1909, is a cantilever bridge crossing the East River from Queens to Manhattan, passing over Roosevelt Island on the way. It's commonly called the 59th Street Bridge because its Manhattan end is located between 59th and 60th streets. Simon and Garfunkel made it famous with their 1966 joyful ditty, "The 59th Street Bridge Song". Even though the song was recorded some 41 years earlier, Paul Simon had the measure of my marathon in his lyrics: "Slow down, you move too fast. Got to make the morning last."

He should have been my coach. I began reciting the song to myself in my head as I pounded westwards towards the skyscrapers and bustle of Mahnattan. From the start of the bridge it looked a short jog onto Manhattan, but the bridge just seemed to go on and on and on.

A cooling breeze blew down the East River, and almost became audible in the spectator-free silence as it swirled around and caressed the criss-crossed ironworks of the bridge structure. The slapping of a myriad shoes on suspended concrete gave the impression of a sustained round of applause; thousands of runners clapping. Maybe the applause was for the iconic view, or their own protracted efforts, or simply the freedom just to lace on a pair of trainers and run.

The applause clattered through the silence as the bridge started to descend beyond its centre, but Manhattan appeared no closer. In my head Paul Simon mused about the street furniture, "Hello lamp-post, whatcha knowin'?" BOOM, Bump! I bet that when Simon penned the ditty the lamp-post didn't know the plastic portaloo that had recently been parked next to it. The exiting runner rejoined the shoe-applause, probably feeling better then a few minutes earlier when he was trying to run a marathon with a full bladder.

Simon had it mostly right; we *were* all "lookin' for fun and feelin' groovy". We "got no deeds to do, no promises to keep", other than finishing this race. Maybe later we'd be "dappled and drowsy and ready to sleep". "Life, I love you, all is groovy". Genius! "The 59th Street Bridge Song" should be the marathon anthem.

The west end of the bridge descended steeply, and we dropped down towards a thunderous booming noise that resembled a passenger jet taking off. Round a sharp left-hand bend the noise increased, and its source was revealed. Thousands and thousands of people were crammed together, straining over the railings and cheering, screaming, shouting, banging. The sound bounced and echoed between the high buildings. The hairs in the back of my neck stood on end, and yet again my arms got goose bumps. This was frighteningly exciting, elation causing, indescribably wonderful. My ears were ringing but I was grinning like the Cheshire Cat. I wondered if this is what it sounds like to score a goal in the cup final at Wembley, or catch the ball and run into the end zone for a Superbowl touchdown.

Another 90-degree left turn launched us onto the wide boulevard of First Avenue for a straight three-and-a-half mile trip northwards to The Bronx. The finish of the race was only nine blocks to the left, but there were ten more miles to run. A glance at my GPS told me I was almost at the seventeen-mile point. Somewhere here would be Andrea, hoping to spot me. Actually I think she was *hoping more* to spot Lance Armstrong, seven times *Tour de France* winner and one of her heroes. We suspected he was running the marathon, but didn't know for certain. If he were, he'd likely be around 20 minutes ahead of me at this point.

I was dearly hoping to see Andrea, partly for a bit of personal support but also to check that she was OK as she'd been on her own all day. But how the heck would I see her with thousands of people straining at the barriers? I only knew she would be near the seventeen-mile point. I was looking for anything that might provide a clue – perhaps a banner with the logo of the sports tour company with which we had travelled – but there was nothing, just a mass of people and a lot of noise.

Another GPS check, I'd run 16.9 miles. Then I saw the official 17-

mile marker, and ran past it. After a few more minutes I checked again, 17.6 miles. My heart sank. I had missed her. Maybe she'd been there as I ran past. Maybe she'd shouted and waved and I just didn't know. Sad though this thought was, I could do nothing but continue, and tried to focus on running to the end.

Something caught my senses, something subliminal, almost imperceptible. Like a lamb recognising its mother's bleat across a crowded flock I sensed a shout of "Matt!" I spun my head round. "Matt, Matt!"

It was Andrea, standing against the barriers about 20 feet behind me to the left. I'd passed her, and was in a tide of runners with no easy way to stop. Remembering my driving lessons I opted to use 'mirror, signal, and manoeuvre'. Quickly glancing all around I looked for the best gap, raised an arm above my head for everyone behind me to see, and then made a dramatic swerve to my left and up against the railings. I then shimmied my way back along the barrier to where Andrea was leaning over, and we embraced with a firm, loving hug. This produced a chorus of "*Aaaaaahhhhhh*" from the nearby crowd.

We were delighted to have seen each other, but there was a race to be run, so we loosened our grip and I made to set off. Andrea stopped me. "*Picture, picture*", she said frantically and pulled out her camera. While the race flooded past, I stood and posed.

And posed......

And posed......

"Come on!" I blurted. "Don't you know there's a race on?"

"Sorry, I forgot to switch the camera on," came the reply, followed by a flash.

The picture taken, I set off again, heading northwards on the left side of First Avenue, with just over eight miles left to the finish, still clutching the last gel sachet in my hand. Oh yes, the gel sachet! I ripped the top off the packet and squirted nectar into my mouth. I hoped this would see me to the finish. There's nothing wrong with a bit of hope.

The GPS was still registering a speed faster than seven minutes per mile as I approached a drinks station in Manhattan's Upper East Side, a few blocks away from the Guggenheim Museum we'd visited the previous afternoon. The first inkling that things were coming unstuck was when I had the desire to lay down at the drinks station and have one of the Gatorade people pour gallons of the stuff into my wide-open mouth. Hmmm, I was thirsty. And come to think of it, my legs seemed a little low on power compared with a couple of miles back. Still, not far to go now, just a short jog.

I risked the sticky shower and grabbed a cup of Gatorade at the aid station, slowing to drink it more easily. Man! That tasted good. Then I grabbed a cup of water and did the same. That was gulped down quickly as well. Just up the road was a bunch of people handing out free PowerGel sachets. This was the 'PowerGel EnergyZone', their advertising stating that it was 'designed to help fuel runners through the wall'.

"No harm in taking one of those as I pass," I thought, grabbing one with my right hand. Then I endeavoured to regain my rhythm and focus on the finish. But groaning and grinding noises began to arise from deep inside my engine. A check of my time on crossing the 30km sensor showed the first signs of slowing, worryingly without trying to.

For the first time my split for the previous 5km had dropped to 23 minutes. Metaphorical bricks were cementing together and slowly dropping into my trainers, threatening to turn them into concrete boots. Still on First Avenue, I ran past Jefferson Park, and then across Willis Avenue Bridge and into The Bronx, trying to ignore the warning sirens blaring from my weakening legs.

Sensible and Reckless had another frank chat:

Sensible: What did I tell you? It's going to happen isn't it? Too fast, too soon!

Reckless: We'll be fine, we're nearly there. Oh, look, there's a Rap band.

Sure enough, on the right hand side of the road stood a woman with a microphone, holding it with the handle through her middle two fingers, in the style only rappers can adopt without looking like an idiot. Heavy beat music thudded through everyone and everything around, and the woman spoke to the rhythm using words that mostly I couldn't interpret. The general gist seemed to be to welcome us runners to The Bronx.

Sensible: Never mind the Rap band, you've gone and pushed too hard. We're going to crash.

Reckless: Stop worrying, keep going. YeeeeHaaaa. Oh look, there's a giant TV screen with all the runners on as they pass. Smile, I bet we look great.

Sure enough, there was a huge monitor directly ahead of us, showing the approaching runners, who all made a right turn from East 138th Street onto Morris Avenue immediately before the screen. I picked myself out in the picture, and tried to smile as I took my turn for the TV flypast. I was shocked to see how bad I looked. The running style was fluid and smooth, but the expression on my face was one of blank emptiness, black holes where my eyes should have been.

Sensible: Did you see that? We look terrible. What have you done?

Reckless: For goodness sake, stop being a pansy. We're nearly there. The legs are fine.

Legs chipped in: Erm...actually...we could do with a bit of help down here. Has anyone got a stretcher?

Sensible: Oh God!

We ran round another three corners before reaching Madison Avenue Bridge, which crosses the Harlem River, heading back onto Manhattan. On the bridge I saw a runner who looked of South American descent, wearing a yellow vest. He suddenly slowed dramatically. Then he began to weave randomly around the road. His wall was a fantastic, monumental, armour-plated, concrete and titanium construction. He'd clearly built this over the last 21 miles, using the finest materials, and it stood there in front of him, totally impenetrable. He weaved a few more times, then tilted to the right, failed to correct his balance, staggered uncontrollably up the kerb onto the sidewalk and straight into the railings on the side of the bridge.

He bounced back into the road directly in front of me, and staggered some more, somehow managing to stay upright despite having suddenly swapped his athletic legs for those of a very drunken man. He fought hard, but his wall fought harder. Fortunately there were two cops standing by. One of them saw his dramatic demise and managed to grab hold of him before he completely lost consciousness. As I passed, the cop was lowering him to the ground whilst calling on his radio for assistance. Yellow Vest himself had a thousand-yard stare and the look of a cartoon character who had been whacked on the head by an anvil, producing a halo of tweeting birds. His race was over.

I was now into Harlem and heading back southwards on Fifth Avenue towards Marcus Garvey Park. I felt to be still moving pretty well but the GPS told an ominous story. The 35km red mat appeared and the frenzied Morse beeps sounded. I was putting in more effort than at any time during the race so far, suffering more pain from pretty much everywhere, yet struggling to maintain a steady pace. The previous 5km took almost 24 minutes. I was grinding to a halt. Glycogen levels were depleted. My batteries were flat. There was more effort but less output, more lead in the boots, more bricks cemented in front of me.

Warning lights flashed right across the dashboard in my brain, and a klaxon sounded in my ears, telling me that non-vital functions were preparing to shut down. I had four-and-a-bit miles to go on an empty tank. Four-and-a-bit miles of pain and torment. Four-and-a-bit miles of 'never again', of regretting filling in the race entry form, of wishing my alarm call had failed that morning and I had stayed in bed. Four-and-a-bit miles of wishing that *Sensible* had given *Reckless* a damned good thumping, and had shut him up at the start.

They say a marathon is run in the last six miles. The old joke goes:

What do you call the 20-mile point of a marathon? Half way! How right. How bloody, painfully, annoyingly right!

After running anti-clockwise around Marcus Garvey Park we hit Fifth Avenue again, and headed southwards for Central Park. The road was initially flat, but then it kicked upwards. It wasn't steep, and certainly nowhere like the hills back home, but with an empty tank there was just not enough power left to drive me onwards. I felt terrible, and by the time we were alongside Central Park my vision started to get hazy. Runners began streaming past me. I'd rampaged through the first half on 'buy now pay later'. Now it was time to pay, with interest.

I was forced to take a short walk break, only for thirty seconds or so, to try and regroup mentally and physically. Over to my left a runner came past, shouting encouragement to a small cluster of followers who were hanging on to his steps like baby animals following their mother. He had an orange balloon tied to him, and he was holding aloft a small baton on which was written "Sub 3:15". He was one of the organised pace-runners, and it was his job to help cajole and generally encourage his group to the finish within their target time of three hours and fifteen minutes. "Hey, that's my target time," I thought and tried to speed up and join his flock. No chance! I ground back to my slow plod.

Sensible: You bloody idiot, Reckless. What did I tell you! You've messed it up.
Reckless: Aw, shut up!!

And with that Reckless sulked away, leaving me to sort out the painful mess he had caused. Still, only three miles to go. How hard could that be? Very hard, as it happens.

I tried to numb the pain by distracting my mind and looking for the Guggenheim Museum, but I didn't see it. Maybe I'd already passed it. The repeated glances to my left just made me realise how slowly I was now running. I tried to peer up ahead to see orange-balloon-3:15 man, but he was out of sight by the time I made the right turn into Central

Park on 86th Street. The lane through the Park was significantly narrower than Fifth Avenue, and it became more crowded as a result. I tried to stay close to the right hand side as I was now haemorrhaging places. The whole world seemed to be passing me. My life story had gone into slow motion while the rest of the universe was on fast forward. It felt that if things continued the same way I'd be so far behind that I'd finish just in time to win next year's race.

Staying close to the right hand edge should have been easy. The lane meandered slightly, but so did I, and unfortunately my wobbly-legged meanderings were out of synchronisation with the tarmac, resulting in me getting in the way of a few faster finishers. It all began to feel like one of those dreams where you are being chased by some hideous monster, and are trying desperately to run away only to find that your legs have completely lost all their strength - despite maximum effort you are barely moving at all. Added to that there was now a painful buzzing in my head and that all too familiar wave of nausea began to rise in the back of my throat and squirm deep in my stomach.

Welcome, once again, to the Bonk!

With spectacular and ruthless efficiency my recklessness had built the wall, and within a stone's throw of the finish I had hit it head on. I prayed I wouldn't be joining Yellow Vest in the back of an ambulance.

Another drink station appeared just past *The Lake* and *Conservatory Water*. I took a cup of Gatorade and glugged it down while walking. Then I took another cup and did exactly the same, and then a cup of water. The feeling of drinking was divine, but completely swamped by the diffuse pain and discomfort, like the pointless exercise of throwing a cup of water on to a burning building.

Full effort got me slow motion running again, reminiscent of *Chariots of Fire*, but devoid of any glory. I managed to keep moving on downhill sections, although somewhat jerkily and painfully, and somehow got to the brow of each uphill section without falling back down.

The crowd of spectators was still huge and very noisy, still held back by barriers, and there were still many shouts of *"Go England!"* and *"Yeah*

Britain!" I tried to wave back to all those cheering me along, but from my wretched appearance and clumsy gesticulating they might have mistakenly thought that I was insulting them. One immaculately dressed chap peered at my shorts, and then spoke in a loud, posh and very proper English accent, "Oh I say, Great Britain! Well done sir." This made me smile, and I gave him a big beaming grin and a thumbs-up as I passed.

Grin became grimace within a dozen paces. English Man's entertaining words segued into those of Mike Gratton from the morning of the group practice run, "Keep some energy in reserve for the last five miles, because you'll need it".

How right he was. How very, very right!

My initial worry that the course was too flat now proved to be a load of codswallop. All I wanted was for the road to be pancake-flat. Actually, that's a lie. All I really wanted was for the finish line to be no more than two steps away, and downhill. But as it was more than two miles away, I just had to get on with it.

The crowds were helping enormously. My legs screamed "Stop, please stop", but spectators yelled "Run, keep going". My pride was cracking the whip and making my legs push harder. It was like thrashing a dying horse, and the horsepower was dying. At the 40km point the last 5km split of the race ticked in at nearly 27 minutes. I was giving it everything and taking over a minute per kilometre longer than in the first part of the race when I was cruising comfortably.

Somehow I managed to hang on and wobbled agonisingly on to the corner of Central Park South. Amazingly, with less than a mile to go, the 'sheep bleat' happened again and something unknown caused me to look into the crowds to my left. Trying to squeeze herself to the front was Andrea. This time the encounter was brief and I didn't stop, but I raised an arm in a pathetic wave before hobbling onwards. (She said afterwards that I looked awful.)

The road rose slightly towards St Columbus Circle, but 'slightly' felt like 'severely' and I needed another walk break. Spectators screamed at me to "Go, go, go! Don't stop, you're nearly there! Run for home!" and my favourite ludicrous shout of the day, "Pain is temporary, glory is forever!" Stuff the glory! In fact, stuff the pain for that matter. If only I had more fuel in my muscles I'd be cruising home. In fact, I'd have already finished.

A shiny glint caught the corner of my eye as my arms swung wearily. I saw the gel sachet still clasped in my right hand where I had grabbed it from the PowerBar people. How stupid was I? I had run carrying this damned gel for seven miles, most of which was unnecessarily, agonisingly tough due to depleted energy reserves, and there, right in my stupid, sweating palm were a few hundred calories.

OK, so one gel sachet wasn't going to plug the giant hole in a sinking ship, but it could have given me a brief sugar hit and made me feel better for a few minutes before the ship sank. But it couldn't do that while still in the packet. Clearly I had learned nothing from my last painful, nauseating mega-bonk when I wobbled through the darkening Chatsworth tunnel with a gel sachet in my bum-bag.

With less than half a mile to go I repeated the Chatsworth debacle and performed the futile deed of squirting the gel into my very appreciative mouth, knowing that it would be of absolutely no help whatsoever. But it felt good, and at least I didn't have to carry it anymore.

The walk break lasted only a few steps before I realised that walking was just as painful as running, but slower. To cheers from the spectators I sped up again, determined to make it running all the way to the finish. Columbus Circle was reached quickly, and a sharp right turn took us back into Central Park at 59th Street, with just 500 yards to the finish. I kept the effort high down the gentle slope, turned a slight left, and could suddenly see the temporary grandstands at the top of the little rise alongside the finishing straight.

Every runner ahead of me appeared to make some effort to please the roaring crowd – some sprinted for all they were worth, others showboated, arms out, aeroplane style, weaving around and waving. Not being the showboat kind, I attempted a sprint finish, but my sprint had finished in Harlem.

As soon as I tried to blast for the line my right hamstring cramped up, and instead of speeding up I hobbled, slowed and limped painfully. Damn! Forced into easing off again I was condemned to the *slowboat* option, but even that was a half hearted and sullen affair, both arms simply raised more in blessed relief than triumph. I crossed the line like the final flight of the *Memphis Belle* – both engines on fire, fuselage ripped and the pilot desperately trying to keep everything the right way up. But I had finished!

I checked the time. Then I double-checked it. I could barely believe it. Despite a head-on crash into a mighty fine wall, hauling my tortured body through a four-mile bonk, and haemorrhaging over six minutes more than expected in the last three miles, the clock on the finishing gantry told me I had run the race in three hours and sixteen minutes. That was only one minute off my target time.

Sixty lousy seconds! Who could I blame for that wretched minute – Andrea for fiddling with the camera, or the high-fiving female Cop who'd tried to slap me all the way back to Staten Island? The truth is, if I'd set off with the wisdom of an owl rather than that of a lemming I would have crushed 3:15.

I should have known better. That wasn't how Mad Dog had taught me to run. However, I was as surprised as I was pleased with the time but, more than that, I was trying very hard not to expire. My experience of big bonks is that the pain doesn't go away just because the running stops. Suffering continues for quite some time as the victimised body takes its vindictive revenge on the mind that subjected it to the torture, torment and general abusive excesses. This bonk was to be no different.

***

Buckaroo

The marshals in the finishing area were super-efficient. They had to shepherd 39,000 people through the narrow lane, past the baggage collection area and out into the reunion areas on Central Park West. I was denied the highly attractive opportunity of curling up and dying just beyond the finish line. Instead I was gently ushered forwards ten yards to an area in front of a banner where someone with a big grin hung a rather fine medal round my neck and yelled "Good job", and a photographer took a picture. I gave it my best 'I'm-not-really-dying' smile, but the shot will probably be used for the promotion of some future zombie film.

I was then wrapped me in a large sheet of cooking foil. Was I being prepared for roasting like an oven-ready turkey? If someone else had approached me bearing sage and onion I would have been extremely worried, but probably unable to resist my stuffing fate. In fact, the foil blanket was a very smart, silver and blue affair, adorned with the New York Marathon logo, and designed to prevent my losing vital body heat and going into a post-exercise hypothermic state. The silver beautifully matched the ghostly pallid colour of my face while the blue was almost exactly the same azure shade as my deathly-looking lips.

Still dehydrated and bonking badly I was ushered further down the lane. Someone wearing latex gloves and a red vest stared at me from a few yards away, seeming to peer deep into my eyes and watch me as I walked forwards. A bit further another red-vested person did the same. Gloved-up and staring at me! Were these the Paxo men? Should I panic? My sphincter tightened.

I eventually realised they were medically trained staff whose job it was to assess every finisher, spot the ones in distress or imminent danger of collapse, and administer appropriate timely first-aid treatment. The fact that they didn't pounce on me and drag me to the nearest emergency unit for urgent cardio-respiratory intervention made me realise that there must have been a whole crowd of people in a worse condition than I was. Lord, have mercy on their souls.

I was handed a bottle of orange sports drink, opened the top but was unable to swallow any due to nausea. I also took a bottle of water from someone else, and then another bottle of water, of which I managed one small mouthful. Someone passed me a bagel, and then I received a chewy sports bar. Freebies were coming thick and fast, and I was rapidly weighing myself down with an array of foodstuffs and heavy, undrinkable beverages that my mouth refused in its sulking state to accept.

No one informed me about this extra challenge that I would face. The freebie peddlers were turning me into a living game of *Buckaroo* (in which I was doing very well – I hadn't dropped anything so far). I felt like shouting "I've just run a bloody marathon, for God's sake. I didn't know I had entered '*It's a Knockout*' as well."

The desire to sit down was overwhelming and, with both hands full, I managed a few paces beyond the last marshal and parked myself on the kerb next to another guy who appeared to be in exactly the same predicament – a picture of pain and a pile of provisions. He had his head in his hands rather than his freebies which were neatly piled next to him. There was empathy between us although neither acknowledged the other. I didn't even know his nationality. There was also a palpable sense of relief that neither of us was the man lying head first in the bushes on the other side of the lane. He was a humorously tragic sight - and sound. Most of his torso was under the bush so that only his legs were visible. We knew he was still alive by the regular vomiting noises arising from deep within the foliage. Welcome to Club Bonk! Membership is free. Only the foolish need apply.

After five minutes sitting, the pain had not eased at all. What was it Mr Springsteen had yelled at me at the start? "You end up like a dog that's been beat too much." Yeah, thanks for that, Bruce.

The stream of foil-wrapped runners ambling past was steadily increasing in number, each one balancing bottles and bagels in their arms like well-deserved spoils of war. It was a bizarre spectacle, a constant convoy of shiny, rustling athletes walking unsteadily with thin legs sticking out of the bottom of the billowing, glistening blankets. Pained expressions had replaced the previously determined stares of the stampede, transmuting it more into a procession of turkeys marching towards Christmas.

Despite feeling that every other runner in the world had passed me in the last few miles, those of us who had already completed the run made up much less than ten per cent of the total number of competitors in the race. Soon the floodgates would open as the masses of middle-of-the-pack runners swamped through the finish area. Much as I would have liked to lie there for an hour or two, I risked being trampled under thousands of trainers. I had only managed a few sips of drink while watching the vomiting bush, but I felt I had to move on.

I abandoned my unnamed bonk buddy, sitting next to me, head still in hands, and stood up again. Andrea would be walking to meet me, and wouldn't have had far to go from where I last saw her. Still strangely unwilling to forgo my freebies I deftly reloaded *Buckaroo* and joined the oven-ready ramble rustling along the road towards the line of UPS vans near Strawberry Fields.

The vans were once again arranged by race bib-number. My van was only the fourth or fifth along. After checking my number the attendant disappeared inside and returned no more than a couple of seconds later with my bag. This also contained drinks – a bottle of post-race recovery drink, and another free bottle of water collected from the start village. *Buckaroo* was ready to kick, so to make things simpler I stuffed all my new freebies in the bag. After hauling my ludicrously heavy swag bag over my shoulder I found a lane leading onto Central Park West.

The avenue had been turned into a long collection area where runners could meet their loved ones. Large signs spaced a block apart were labelled alphabetically. This enabled people to leave westwards along each of the streets joining Central Park West. I staggered through the growing crowd down the avenue, heading towards the end sign which was for runners with surnames beginning with 'A' or 'B'. There were far more relatives and spectators than finished runners. A few people congratulated me as I made my way, the foil blanket round my shoulders and bronze coloured medal dangling from my neck making me feel like a walking Christmas tree.

I arrived under the 'A+B' sign feeling just as wretched as the moment I had finished, and looked eagerly around for Andrea. She was nowhere to be seen. Still nauseous, I slumped down and sat in the road, waiting. Knowing that re-hydration was a priority I reached into my bag and rummaged through the wide selection of drinks.

Several gulps of sports drink were forced through pursed lips and down a throat that wobbled objectionably. Thankfully the drink stayed down. And so did I. Down on the tarmac was the place to be, at one with gravity, nowhere to fall from there.

"Excuse me? Are you OK?" The woman looked down at me in a concerned manner.

"Erm, not too bad, thanks," I lied.

"Oh, good. I just thought I'd check. You looked a bit...uncomfortable."

Strange use of the word uncomfortable, I thought. Uncomfortable was obviously a diplomatic euphemism for 'hideous'.

She spoke with an English accent, and as we chatted she informed me that they were from Nottingham and that her husband was running. I had just explained that I was waiting for my wife when Andrea appeared, looked down at me and grimaced. Ever supportive, and forthcoming with the truth, she gave me a big hug while describing how awful I looked - white face, blue lips, vacant empty stare. (She was right. I've seen the pictures.)

The chilly November air began to nip at my damp, sweaty skin. I'd put my lightweight running jacket on under the foil blanket, but I was cooling fast and needed to get back to the hotel to warm up. Standing, but still wobbly, I said goodbye to 'Nottingham lady' and started walking. I'd hardly recovered and Andrea suggested a taxi ride. Central Park West was closed to traffic; there were no taxis nearby. As luck would have it a bicycle taxi (a man riding a bike with a two-seater trailer attached) was waiting on the corner of 69th Street. Andrea suggested we ride with him. I didn't object.

As the rider pulled away, I asked Andrea whether she'd seen Lance Armstrong. She hadn't and looked genuinely disappointed. Lance was an icon to us, not only because of his unprecedented *Tour de France* career but also for his own personal cancer story. Before any of his Tour victories Lance was diagnosed with testicular cancer. By then the disease had already spread to his brain and lungs. His fight and recovery was the stuff of legend.

After his battle, he founded the Lance Armstrong Foundation, *Livestrong*, whose mission is to "unite people to fight cancer believing that unity is strength, knowledge is power and attitude is everything".

Andrea was pleased, however, to have seen Paula Radcliffe steaming along at the front of the women's race, with Gete Wami hot on her heels. Andrea screamed encouragement to fellow Brit, Paula, and was delighted to hear that she had won. The Kenyan, Martin Lel, won the men's race.

The breeze on the back of the bike sliced through the foil, freezing the turkey into goose bumps (again, but for a different reason this time), but the ride was such a white knuckle one that I barely noticed. That cyclist was a *kamikaze*, cutting through traffic in a manner that the yellow cabs would consider suicidal, running red lights, swerving in front of lorries, weaving through the narrowest of gaps in the moving traffic. I was even whiter by the time his brakes squealed to a stop outside the Crowne Plaza, but he certainly got us there quickly.

We paid the fare, added a generous tip, and he took a photograph of us both sitting in the back of his bike before a painful dismount had me back on my feet. Still ready for the oven I walked back through the hotel lobby, back into the rocket elevator, and we blasted up through 31 floors.

The cup of tea and biscuits were exquisite, the sports drinks were exquisite, the hot bath was exquisite (and this time I was extra cautious not to drown in it), and the long lie down on the bed was the most exquisite of all. Shakespeare's Hamlet said, "Nothing is good or bad.

Thinking only makes it so". Without bad there could be no good; there would be no comparison to make.

Looking out of the hotel room window into Times Square, there couldn't have been a greater contrast with the hills and moorland, and the isolation of the running back home. Life is full of contrasts, to be celebrated and enjoyed, anticipated and endured. There are many things to run from in this world, but even more to run toward.

There we were in the middle of corporate, capitalist, money-driven, ultra-marketed, hi-tech America. Everyone had everything. Neon flashed all around, trying to get us to spend money, to look right, to buy right, to have right, eat right, want right, wear right, drive right, work right...Yet the simple things in life – a bath, a bed, and a cup of tea made by someone you love – are worth far more than the finest material riches.

It all somehow reminded me of the first few lines of John Hodge's depressing and hard-hitting poem that featured at the start of the film *Trainspotting*: "Choose Life. Choose a job. Choose a career. Choose a f****** big television, choose washing machines, cars, compact disc players and electrical tin openers..." In the film the character Renton chose *not* to choose life. He chose heroin: a bad choice.

I chose running.

On returning home to England I logged on to the New York marathon website to check the official timing-chip results. The multinational nature of the event was clear to see; the finishers around me included runners from France, Japan, The Netherlands, Italy, Switzerland, Germany, Canada, Denmark, Venezuela, Morocco, South Korea, and of course the United States.

My particular statistics showed what I already knew. My average pace was very close to what I'd hoped for, at exactly seven minutes and 30 seconds per mile. But each 5km split showed a progressive slowing: 21:30, 21:42, 22:05, 22:27, 22:43, 23:16, 24:57, and 26:46.

Lance Armstrong had indeed run the race, and finished in a time of two hours 46 minutes.

The New York trip had been fantastic, but the high point was the simple act of running until it hurt, then being eased through the pain by the person I loved, just as I had tried to ease her through her torment earlier in the year. Materialism and consumerism didn't matter a fig. We had shared our pains, and we shared the pleasures. In this context, the New York Marathon experience was both colossal and humbling.

Andrea and I still woke up every morning, and the roller coaster rumbled onwards, taking us on the ride of our lives through twists and turns unknown, over peaks of fantastic height, and into troughs of mysterious depth.

But what of the cancer battle? Had the war been won? Had the surgery and the drugs extracted and eliminated the evil? Or was some lumbering beast following us, chasing us, stalking, waiting silently to strike again? There was no way to know. Regular check-ups with Dr Purohit and yearly mammograms would help, but the only thing to do was to keep running and never look back. That was how we lived.

Life on the run.

The day before the New York Marathon. The start of the final 385 yards in Central Park.......

.......and the finish-line grandstands.

The mid-race photograph at mile 17, First Avenue, Manhattan.

Finished and on the ground on Central Park West.

Arriving in Times Square at the end of the bicycle taxi ride.

In both running and life there are moments when it feels almost easy, and there are moments when you have to fight deep within yourself just to stand still - but if we run and we live with love - then more becomes possible than we ever might have dreamed.

Lizzy Hawker

<u>Victory</u>

Sunday 14th December 2008

With three hundred yards to go, she kicked for home, and I was forced to run hard just to hang on to her pace. I had been trying to hide my tears for the last mile. I never knew she had such speed in her, especially going uphill after her longest ever run. She whirled around the final left-hand bend like a mad woman, and went hell-for-leather for the line while I sprinted as closely behind as I could, making sure nobody would split us at the finish.

For an hour Andrea had been chasing her demons, rounding them up, hunting them down. I'd run alongside her all the way. Where else could I have been? With 50 yards to go, she had them all cornered, and there was no escape. She blasted through the finish, and in doing so she'd swung a mighty sword and slain the whole army of demons that had tortured her for the last two years.

Then the pent-up fear, frustration, anger and helplessness inevitably exploded in an outburst of pure and intense emotion. She was crying so hard and breathing so hard, doing neither properly; she jerked and sobbed in my arms while a gallon of tears washed down her reddened face. I wondered if she'd ever breathe properly again. I was in no better state – sobbing intensely, trying to catch my breath, and hugging her like I was never going to let go.

Some of the marshals and other finishers at the 2008 Bolsover 10k watched us, wondering what the hell was going on; why were two people who had just finished an average local event in 688th and 689th place standing in a sobbing embrace? But we were oblivious to them.

Hundreds of runners had finished ahead of us, but today Andrea had won the most important race in the world.

The goal recedes ever from us. The greater the progress, the greater the recognition of our unworthiness. Satisfaction lies in the effort, not in the attainment. Full effort is full victory.

Mahatma Gandhi

Epilogue

Onwards and upwards.

There's no other way to go. Life deals the cards, and we have no choice but to play our hand to the best of our ability. Sometimes things are tough, and you have to stick it out, or bluff it out. But never fold. In the words of Winston Churchill, "If you're going through Hell, keep going".

Andrea kept going. Every successive follow-up with Dr Purohit's team led one step further towards reassurance. But every subsequent pain, ache and feeling of tiredness brought with it the fear that it may be time to take up the unwanted fight once again. Thankfully, so far those fears have proved unfounded and they slowly diminish with passing time.

The Bolsover 10K race remains a regular target for Andrea. Each crossing of the finish line is an emotional moment. Our lives could have been very different. The cancer battle made us reassess our priorities, and made us realise what we have and how lucky we are.

But what of my running adventures?

Well, Mad Dog once suggested that in my mind I was 'condemned to be an ultra-runner'. As always, he was right.

The North York Moors seemed to become a perennial battleground for my challenges. In 2008 I had a disastrous run in the official Lyke Wake race. After contracting food poisoning and vomiting several times before half way, my race was doomed. But I pressed on in a 'death or glory' attempt at finishing - against all the odds and against all sense.

Needless to say, the experience was ghastly.

The eternal question, "How far *could* I run?", hung like a millstone around my neck. In 2009 team Respect the Stupidity went to stupendous lengths to try and find out. The memories of tackling the Cleveland Way race are vivid - running all through the night, all the next day, and continuing into the second night, and then Justin phoning for an ambulance as I lay at Mal and Vin's feet, desperately trying to soak up the coldness of the ground in a vain attempt to extinguish the inferno raging deep within my body.

The *Hardmoors 110* had been exactly as the name sounds. I had annihilated my previous best single run distance, and done very well in the race.

But at a price.........

Appendix

The Lyke Wake Dirge

Traditional version: Rough translation:

This yah neet, this yah neet ,   This night, this night,
- Ivvery neet an' all,   - every night as well,
Fire an' fleet an' cannle leet,   Fire and ember and candle light,

An' Christ tak up thy saul.   And Christ take your soul.

When thoo frae hence away art passed,   When you have passed away from here,

- Ivvery neet an' all,   - every night as well,
Ti Whinny Moor thoo cums at last,   To Whinny Moor you come at last,

An' Christ tak up thy saul.   And Christ take your soul.

If ivver thoo gav owther hosen or shoon,   If you ever gave someone clothes or shoes,

- Ivvery neet an' all,   - every night as well,
Clap thee doon, an' put 'em on,   Sit down and put them on,
An' Christ tak up thy saul.   And Christ take your soul.

Bud if hosen an' shoon thoo nivver gav neean,   But if you never gave any clothes or shoes,

- Ivvery neet an' all,   - every night as well,
T'whinnies'll prick thee sair ti t'beean,   The Whinnies will prick you to the bone,

An' Christ tak up thy saul.   And Christ take your soul.

235

Frae *Whinny Moor* *when thoo art passed,*

- Ivvery neet an' all,
Ti t'Brig o' Dreead tho cums at last,

 •

An' Christ tak up thy saul.

If ivver thoo gav o' thy siller an' gowd,
- Ivvery neet an' all,
On t'Brig o'Dreead thoo'll finnd footho'd,

An' Christ tak up thy saul.

Bud if silver an' gowd thoo nivver gav neean,

- Ivvery neet an' all,
Thoo'll doon, doon tumle towards Hell fleeame,

An' Christ tak up thy saul.

Frae t'Brig o' Dreead when thoo art passed,

- Ivvery neet an' all,
Ti t'fleeames o' Hell tho'll cum at last,

An' Christ tak up thy saul.

If ivver thoo gav owther bite or sup,

- Ivvery neet an' all,
T'fleeames'll nivver catch thee up,

When you have passed from
Whinny Moor,

- every night as well,
To the Brig of Dread you will
come at last,

And Christ take your soul.

If you ever gave silver or gold,
- every night as well,
You'll find a foothold on the
Brig of Dread,

And Christ take your soul.

But if you never gave any silver
or gold,
- every night as well,
You'll tumble down towards
Hell's flame,

And Christ take your soul.

When you have passed from
the Brig of Dread,
- every night as well,
To the flames of Hell you'll
come at last,

And Christ take your soul.

If you ever gave someone food
or drink,
- every night as well,
The flames will never catch you
up,

An' Christ tak up thy saul.	And Christ take your soul.
Bud if bite or sup thoo nivver gav neean,	But if you never gave any food or drink,
- Ivvery neet an' all,	- every night as well,
T' flames'll bon thee sair ti t'beean,	The flames will burn you to the bone,
An' Christ tak up thy saul.	And Christ take your soul.
This yah neet, this yah neet ,	This night, this night,
- Ivvery neet an' all,	- every night as well,
Fire an' fleet an' cannle leet,	Fire and ember and candle light,
An' Christ tak up thy saul.	And Christ take your soul.

(Traditional version from www.lykewake.org/dirge.php)

Useful Links:

Mad Dog www.training2run.com

The Running Bug www.therunningbug.co.uk

209 Events www.209events.com

Lizzy Hawker www.lizzyhawker.com

Lizzy Hawker www.laufschule-scuol.ch

Get ultra running www.getultrarunning.eu

Mud Sweat and Tears www.mudsweatandtears.co.uk

Ultrarunner www.ultrarunner.co.uk

New York marathon www.ingnycmarathon.org

NY marathon route
www.realbuzz.com/ingnewyorkcitymarathon/images/coursemap.pdf

The Lyke Wake Walk www.lykewakewalk.co.uk

The Lyke Wake Walk www.lykewake.org

The Chatsworth Challenge www.thechatsworthchallengewalk.co.uk

The Worksop Half Marathon www.worksopharriers.co.uk

The Bolsover 10K www.ndrc.co.uk

North York Moors www.northyorkmoors.org.uk

Peak District www.peakdistrict.gov.uk

Chatsworth www.chatsworth.org